ARTHURIAN STUDIES VI

The Arthurian Bibliography

ARTHURIAN STUDIES

I

ASPECTS OF MALORY

Edited by Toshiyuki Takamiya and Derek Brewer

II

THE ALLITERATIVE MORTE ARTHURE

A Reassessment of the Poem

Edited by Karl Heinz Goller

III

THE ARTHURIAN BIBLIOGRAPHY

I Author Listing

Edited by Cedric E. Pickford and Rex Last

IV

THE CHARACTER OF KING ARTHUR
IN MEDIEVAL LITERATURE

Rosemary Morris

V

PERCEVAL: THE STORY OF THE GRAIL

Chrétien de Troyes
Translated by Nigel Bryant

ISSN 0261-9814

The Arthurian Bibliography

II SUBJECT INDEX

Edited by Cedric E. Pickford and Rex Last

Assistant editor Christine R. Barker

D. S. BREWER

Published for the Eugène Vinaver Fund
by D. S. Brewer, 240 Hills Road, Cambridge
an imprint of Boydell and Brewer Ltd
PO Box 9, Woodbridge, Suffolk IP12 3DF

and by
Biblio
81 Adams Drive, Totowa, N.J. 97512

First published 1983

British Library Cataloguing in Publication Data
Pickford, C. E.
    The Arthurian bibliography. – (Arthurian studies; 6)
    2: Subject index
    1. Arthur, *King* – Bibliography
    I. Title   II. Last, R. W.   III. Barker, Christine R.
    IV. Series
    016.398'352   Z8045
    ISBN 0-85991-099-7

Library of Congress Cataloging in Publication Data
Pickford, Cedric Edward.
    The Arthurian bibliography.

    (Arthurian studies, ISSN 0261-9814 ; 6)
    Contents: -- 2. Subject index.
    1. Arthurian romances -- History and criticism --
Indexes. I. Last, Rex William. II. Barker,
Christine R. III. Title. IV. Series.
Z8045.P53   016.809'93351   83-2579
ISBN 0-85991-099-7 (v. 2)

Printed in Great Britain by
St Edmundsbury Press, Bury St Edmunds, Suffolk

*It is with great regret that
the publishers have to record the death of
Professor Cedric Pickford
just after this volume was passed for press.
The original concept of this project
was due to him, and his untiring energy
made its completion possible.*

INTRODUCTION

When the editors of the present bibliography embarked on the project of generating a computer-assisted bibliography of critical Arthurian literature they were aware that the sheer bulk of the material presented severe constraints and created problems, the solution of which could not necessarily meet all the requirements of all the different users. The arrangement of the material in the annually produced *Bibliographical Bulletin* of the International Arthurian Society, in which each national section published material in the categories (a) texts, translations and adaptations, (b) critical and historical studies, (c) reviews, and (d) dissertations and theses, while offering a splendid account of scholarly work undertaken throughout the world, does not make for ease of reference. Rudolf Brummer, in his review of *Bulletins No. 8, 9, 10, 11*, published in *Zeitschrift für Romanische Philologie* Vol. 77 (1961) pp. 168-169, made this very point and regretted that the *Bulletin Bibliographique* did not classify the works listed by subject matter. The suggestion tended to overlook the fact that each *Bulletin* does contain, as well as an *Index of Authors*, an *Index of Works and Subject Matter*. To consult some thirty different indexes is not a convenient procedure, but in the case of a composite bibliography, the compiling of a subject index seemed at first sight to be a logical and convenient way of presenting the material.

Before adopting this procedure we examined other possibilities. The need for comprehensive bibliographies was beginning to be met by the publication of *Research Bibliographies and Check Lists* by Grant and Cutler of London. The first to appear, *Hispanic Arthurian Material I, Texts of the Prose Romance Cycles*, by Harvey L. Sharrer (1977), deals with a relatively small area, but even so is subdivided into five main sections comprising in all twenty-three sub-sections. That devoted to a much larger topic - *Chrétien de Troyes*, by Douglas Kelly (1977), consists of twenty-one main sections, made up of a total of ninety sub-sections. Glynn Burgess's *Marie de France Bibliography* (1977), contains 529 items in five main sections and David Shirt's *Bibliography of The Old French Tristan Poems* reverts to the system of main sections (11) and sub-sections (73). The method of presentation and classification of the material in these excellent research tools varies slightly to suit the different subjects of the bibliographies.

These bibliographies deal of course with selected aspects of Arthurian literature. The problems of classification and ordering which arise when one handles a range of topics - let alone the whole gamut of Arthurian criticism - increase dramatically. Broad lines of classification are moderately easy to determine at first sight, but questions arise immediately the bibliographer considers detail. Should works be considered on the basis of the language in which the mediaeval texts were written - Welsh, French, German, to name but a few - or on the basis of themes or genres - the *Tristan* legend, the verse romances, the prose romances? Where are comparative studies to be placed? How are works whose authorship is unknown to be listed? What is the place for historical, iconographical or archaeological studies? Much conveniently arranged bibliographical information is to be found in the footnotes to the collaborative history of *Arthurian Literature in the Middle Ages (ALMA)*, but it is far from being an extensive repertoire of titles. Again, J. D. Bruce, especially in the second edition of his *Evolution of Arthurian Romance*, provides a good basic framework in the final chapter of Part VII - *A Select Bibliography of Arthurian Critical Literature* (Vol.II, pp. 380-412), to which should be added the *Bibliographical Supplement* by Alfons Hilka (Vol. II, pp. 445-460). Repetition of items which treat more than one topic adds to the bulk of this bibliography, (for example, Wechssler, *Die Sage vom Heiligen Graal* on page 399 under Holy Grail, and page 408 under the Prose Romances). Cross referencing is also necessary. When confronted by the immense volume of scholarly works published since 1928, we realised that a classification system which would inevitably require both extensive repetition of items and a considerable amount of cross referencing would be both exceedingly bulky and at the same time inconvenient to use. Would a more selective approach to the material be a justifiable procedure? To operate a process of selection by eliminating items of less scholarly value would certainly reduce the number of items to be included. We felt that this was not a procedure which could commend itself. How could a small group of editors (in fact three) have the range of expertise to decide what should be excluded and what should be retained? We decided to follow the principle of including all the items which were in the sources which we used. One result of this is that it has been pointed out that some items are 'trash.' That may well be so, but it is better to include what may today be judged unworthy (though in its own day it was well respected) rather than to omit works which could well be of interest to someone working in the field. Value judgements in Arthurian matters are dangerously liable to be highly personal as well as short-lived. In addition, such alleged trivia may well themselves be a genuine object of interest to the researcher.

Our experience of using the various Arthurian bibliographical sources demonstrated to us that the best solution was to adopt a formula not unlike that of *Bibliography of Critical Arthurian Literature for the Years 1922-1929*, prepared by John J. Parry for the American group of the Modern Language Association of America. Here, one single alphabetical listing by author is followed by a subject index.

This therefore became the basic shape of the *Arthurian Bibliography* - two main sectors, a listing by authors followed by an index of works and subject matter. As the preparation of the author listing advanced, we realised that to present the whole simultaneously in one volume would produce a book so thick that it would be impossible to handle. To present it in two volumes - with the subject index in a separate volume - would not merely produce books of manageable proportions, but would greatly facilitate consultation. The decision was therefore taken to produce, as soon as it was ready, the author listing, and to prepare the subject index separately.

Having made this decision, the method of dealing with mediaeval works of literature whose author is not known, or whose attribution is debatable, presented fewer difficulties. To note these works in the author listing under the name of the modern editor, and to place the anonymous works by title in the subject index led logically to the step of treating all mediaeval works in this way. Thus the anonymous *Gawain and the Green Knight*, like the *Yvain* of Chrétien de Troyes is to be found in many different places in the author listing, but in one place only in the subject index. This seemed preferable to treating in the author listing anonymous works under their title - which is illogical in an author listing - and writers such as Malory sometimes as authors on the same footing as modern critics, and sometimes as the subject matter about which modern critics write.

The result of all this is that in the author listing each critical work appears in principle on one occasion only, under the name of the author. There is no repetition and cross-referencing is restricted to multiple authorship or to items in composite volumes (for example, the items in L575 [MLQ '737] Loomis, *Arthurian Literature in the Middle Ages* are listed separately by author and cross-referenced to '737, that is L575).

In this second volume of Index by Subject, items are indexed according to the topics to which they refer, and as fully as the source material has permitted. It is evident that in a bibliography of a specialised kind consisting of over 10,000 entries (if reviews are included) certain topics will be referred to many times. The procedure we have adopted is to try to combine two aims. On the one hand to list all references to a topic under a general heading - for example, *Grail*, and then within that topic introduce sub-headings in which feature more specialised items, which may also be included under the general heading.

The user of this volume of 'yellow pages' turns then to a main heading (for example, Grail) where he is faced by an immense array of references. Beneath that will be found sub-headings. Given the wide range of literatures and languages in which Arthurian themes figure, the general heading inevitably includes many items which do not refer to a particular language or literature, and such references are to be found in the sub-headings.

Where variant spellings, translations of titles, or variant titles could cause confusion, there is cross-referencing. Each reference begins with a letter followed by a number : the letter is that of the alphabetical sequence of the author listing, the number refers to the item within the alphabetical sequence.

During the course of the preparation of the index, we decided that the references to editions of Arthurian texts would be better presented not in the form of a string of numbers but by giving in full the details of the various editions. Our first plan was to divide the index into two parts - (A) Editions and (B) Critical Works. As we proceeded to prepare this listing of editions, we decided that it could usefully form an independent volume. The author listing is as complete as the sources listed on pages XIV and XV of Volume I. We are aware of the fact that since the Bruce bibliography rarely refers to texts written after the year 1300 there are important lacunae of earlier editions, particularly of Middle English and Spanish texts. The Middle English texts listed in Robert W. Ackerman's *Index of Arthurian*

Names in Middle English (A33) are included in the author listing only if they have been reprinted and noted in our sources. For these reasons we deemed it preferable to undertake the listing of editions of Arthurian texts as a separate task, especially since many editions are not noted as such in the sources. A third volume of the bibliography will therefore be devoted to the classified listing of critical editions.

Names of medieval authors, where known (for example, Chretien de Troyes and Marie de France), are presented as main headings, alphabetically listed according to the name by which they are most commonly known. Thus, Chretien de Troyes appears in C, and Wolfram von Eschenbach in W, while Sir Thomas Malory is listed as Malory, Sir Thomas, and Geoffrey Chaucer under Chaucer, Geoffrey. The titles of their works are presented in inverted commas as sub-headings of the author's name, in alphabetical order. Modern authors who themselves are the subject of critical Arthurian literature, or whose works are of interest to Arthurian scholars, are listed alphabetically according to surname, with their works as sub-headings. Thus, Mark Twain's *A Connecticut Yankee at King Arthur's Court* will be found as a subdivision of Twain, Mark.

Names such as King Arthur, King Lear, King Mark, Sir Galahad, Sir Lancelot, etc., are entered in the subject index under their Christian name, with cross-references under 'King' and 'Sir' where necessary. Titles of works appear in inverted comas, either as a subdivision of their author, or standing alone in the appropriate alphabetical sequence. 'Lais' and 'lays' in general appear under the main heading 'Lais, lays', and individual lays are listed according to their usual title, as a subdivision of their author, if known. Thus 'Guigemar' is listed as a subdivision of Marie de France, while 'Lai de Graelent' is listed alphabetically in L, with cross-references in G in both cases. The title of the original language in which the lay was written has been retained, so that whereas 'Lai de Graelent' is listed in the 'Lai' category, 'Lay of the Big Fool' will be found under 'Lay'.

Themes and topics given in the sources under different names and in a variety of languages have been merged together under the most appropriate English heading: for example, items dealing with 'amour courtois' appear under 'Courtly love', and all commemorative and celebratory volumes which appear in the author listing as 'Studies', 'Melanges', etc., are listed under 'Festschriften'.

C. E. Pickford and Christine R. Barker

TECHNICAL INTRODUCTION

The programming involved in the subject index was even more complex than that demanded by the author index. As was the case with the author index, the data from the MLQ and BBSIA indexes was keyed in (by members of the Manpower Services team), edited, and then set on one side until the completion of the author index.

As two of the editors were on the point of moving to Scotland at the time when the author index was nearing completion, there was a difficult problem of timing to be overcome. The mainframe in the University of Dundee, from which this second volume has been produced (with the exception of this introduction, which has been produced on the microcomputer system in the Department of Modern Languages, Dundee), is entirely different from the Hull machine, and a decision had to be taken either to bring the first volume to a rapid conclusion, or to wait for a further year or so until work could recommence on the completion of the first volume (the author index), which itself would bring further delays - if full advantage were taken of the technology currently available - involving the conversion of the entire text to upper and lower case, the provision of diacritics, and marking the whole text for phototypesetting.

The decision was taken to press ahead with the author index, on the grounds that further delays would be unacceptable, but this meant that no computerised cross-checking would be possible between the two indexes. Fate was kind: our hand-checking of the author index was sufficiently rigorous, since, when the programming on the subject index was sufficiently advanced, a full cross-check was undertaken, with the result that only a small handful of items was found to be missing or misplaced. All the substantive errors are noted in this volume; no attempt has been made to deal with the occasional spelling error, or with the lack of conformity in the layout of items (largely occasioned during the years that the BBSIA volumes 'went French'), since the principal objective of the author index was to produce a workshop bibliography from a vast data base with resources in money and manpower terms which were very far from adequate.

The update of the bibliography (BBSIA volumes 31-35), together with the second full edition (planned for ten years hence), will both be phototypeset in upper and lower case, and will, if the appropriate funding becomes available, be completely checked through for inconsistencies.

Work on the subject index fell into a number of stages. The first consisted of a suite of programs designed to check the accuracy of the input data, and it was at this point that the first major problem arose, the familiar one of inconsistencies which rendered a substantial portion of the data incompatible with the rest. Not only were the French-produced indexes linguistically out of step, they also produced spurious items which were merely the titles of the critical works referred to without any attempt properly to categorise them.

In addition, the BBSIA approach to multiple authorship and to the referencing of medieval authors was totally at variance with the rest of the input data, since the BBSIA volumes have two separate indexes, the second of which is the subject index proper, whilst the first lists modern and medieval authors and, in addition, contains many entries superfluous to our requirements, since they itemise the authors of reviews, which (a) seemed to us to offer little of real value to the user, and (b) would have required a massive effort of additional work by hand on the MLQ and other bibliographies if it were decided to refer to all authors of reviews throughout. (If any user requires a list of specific review authors, this can be abstracted from the database. Please contact Professor Last in Dundee University for further information about this and similar enquiries.)

The first checking stage also revealed that a number of items in our source for the author index were omitted from the appropriate original subject index, and that there were a number of duplicate entries.

The next stage of the operation involved an attempt to merge the subject indexes: this had, however, to be broken down into two stages because of the lack of parallel between the MLQ and BBSIA indexes and also because of a very high rate of inconsistency between the way in which the indexes as a whole treated sub-entries beneath the various main headings. It was decided to use the MLQ subject indexes as a base: these were merged together separately, as were the BBSIA entries. Then, employing lengthy editing techniques, the BBSIA index was merged into the MLQ index. (For this purpose, an editing and file-handling program was specially devised, partly in readiness for any subsequent team of assistants to use in succession to the FAG macro written in Hull. The DEC10 mainframe in Dundee demanded an entirely different approach.)

Then a cross-checking program was written which indicated the nature of the subject index reference for each entry in the author index, and this permitted gaps in the original indexes to be filled, and also for the nature of all subject index entries to be monitored and, where necessary, improved. It was at this stage too that the Foley, Takamiya and early BBSIA items placed in the author index were allocated subject index entries, as were medieval author names originally in the BBSIA indexes of names.

In parallel with this process, work was undertaken to ensure that full cross-referencing (i.e. onomastics - names - personal names) was undertaken, and that entries were grouped in 'word fields' under the most obvious headword that could be devised.

At this point it will readily be recognised that the reference numbers in the subject index were, by this time, in a more or less random order. The next stage, therefore, was a routine which sorted the items in order; the opportunity was also taken at this point to right justify the whole text.

The intention had been to output the entire text by means of the Oxford University Lasercomp service (which has been used for the introductions to this edition and will also be employed in the third volume). For a variety of reasons, this would have involved a further delay of several months, so the body of the index is printed, as was the author index, on a Diablo printer.

To jump right out of time sequence: when the magnetic tape containing the subject index first arrived in Dundee, it was run through a program which converted (under programmer control) the text to upper and lower case, preparatory to using the Lasercomp. Although it was decided to revert to the Diablo, the upper and lower case feature was retained, but no diacritics were available. This will be remedied in all cases where the Lasercomp is used in the future.

The last stage was a program which printed the final output, together with page numbering and running heads, on to the Diablo printer. The opportu The production of the author index was expedited by a facility called FAG , which was designed for the non-expert users who was inputting and editing material. This was written in the GEORGE operating system, and the move to Dundee necessitated a complete rewriting of this facility. This was done in SIMULA. Both the programs have roughly the same features: they enable the creation and editing of files to take place on the basis of a question and answer system enabling the naive user to forget about the computer itself and its operating system.

In conclusion, the lessons learned from this project from a programming point of view have been considerable (not least in improving my own programming techniques in a variety of languages and with different operating systems!), but the basic lesson is that of any complex project. If the original design is right, the rest will follow; if the project is taken flexibly a stage at a time, then disaster can be avoided more often. I hope that those who use this Bibliography will recognise the dedicated effort of many years that has been involved, and will be indulgent towards the blemishes which will doubtlessly remain. The real lesson, though, should perhaps be: Never embark on a bibliographical project. What appears at first sight to be the work of months soon spreads into years - and all the time new volumes of the BBSIA bibliography keep appearing, with ever-increasing numbers of entries. But at least we now have within our reach far more powerful technological aids for the inputting, processing and printing of the bibliographical material than the punched cards and upper-case character set we started with ten years ago.

Rex W. Last.

CORRECTIONS

Only substantive corrections are listed here. Page references are given only where no item number exists, otherwise all references are to item numbers in the author listing.

p. xvi nos. 3171-3191 are attributed twice to different items in Vols. XI and XII of MODERN LANGUAGE QUARTERLY, Bibliographies for 1950 and 1951. The author listing uses the numbers as given in the MODERN LANGUAGE QUARTERLY, together with the year reference, i.e. MLQ/1950/3175 is a different item from MLQ/1951/3175.

p. xviii add BAYREUTHER BLAETTER.

p. xxviii add REVUE DES COURS ET CONFERENCES.

p. xxxii add WESTFAELISCHER ERZIEHER.

A17 for BBSIA/VII/40 read BBSIA/VIII/40.

A90 for MLQ/1959/5365 read MLQ/1959/4635.

A151 for ANCIENT SEARCH read ANCIENT SECRET.

p. 17 replace ARBERRY, A.J. SEE IBN HAZM #3648 by
        ARBERRY, A.J., TRANS.
        A235A   [MLQ/1953/3648]
        "THE RING OF THE DOVE", PARIS: LUZAC, 1953.
        REVIEWS ETC.: IN LTLS, JUNE 12, 1953, P. 375;
        BY A.S. TRITTON IN FOLKLORE LXIV 1953, P. 440.

p. 17 for MEYER #1331 read MEYER M424.

A237 for COUNT OF read COUNT OF SAVOY.

A244A after author's name add ED.

B28 this is an edition.

B44 after author's name add ED.

B52 after author's name add ED.

B286 after authors' names add EDS. AND TRANS.

B293A after author's name add AND TRANS.

B320 and B321 after authors' names add EDS.

B371 after author's name add ED.

B435 delete penultimate review.

B440 for BLOCK read BLOCH.

B473 for M.S. read MS.

B702 final line, for PP. 157-77 read PP. 54-85.

B815 for ANGLIA, XXXIII read ANGLIA, XXIII.

p. 96 add B858A   [MLQ/1936/1827]
*   "VERBESSERUNGEN ZUM TEXT UND ERGAENZUNGEN*
*   ZU DEN VARIANTEN DER AUSGABE DER 'PROPHECIES*
*   MERLIN' DES MAISTRE RICHART D'IRLANDE". ZRPH,*
*   LVI 1936, 563-603.*

B894-B900 see also DAVIES, CONSTANCE B.

B901 for BU'LOCK, J.D. read BULLOCK, J.D.

B924 see also SEVERS, J. BURKE S447.

B934 for BBSIA/XVI/175 read BBSIA/XVII/138.

C67 this is an edition.

C189 see also M213.

C190 see also F237.

C195 after author's name add ED.

C216 delete item number but not reviews, which are of C211.

C224 after author's name add ED.

C236 for VERSION BY MALORY read VERSION OF MALORY.

C297 see also R400.

C361 for SAONTE read SAINTE.

D28-D32 see also BULLOCK-DAVIES, CONSTANCE.

D68 see also LEJEUNE, RITA.

D112, line 16 for ARARAMON read ARAMON, and delete last review.

D263 for BBSIA, IX 1957 read BBSIA, IX 1957, 57.

D274 add AND TRANS. after author's name.

D312 add EDMOND after author's name.

E110 for BBSIA/V/100 read BBSIA/V/101, and at end
*   of entry add LISBON: IMPRENSA NACIONAL, 1942.*

E146 REVIEWS add REPLY TO OOKA BY ETO IN ASAHI-SHIMBUN
*   (BUNKA-RAM), 1.12.1975, P. 5 (IN JAPANESE).*

F1 F.,C. = FOULON CHARLES.

F65 add review BY G. DI STEFANO IN SF, XXII 1967, P. 319.

F116 add FIELD, P.J.C., ED.

F290 for GRAAL #4245 read GRAA1 C297.

F356 for CENTURY #5304 read CENTURY U17.

F374 delete J.F.

F388 line 17 for FANCO ANCIENNE read FRANCE ANCIENNE.

F414 replace SUMMARY IN BBSIA, XX, 209 by REV. BY M.
          RICHTER IN SF, XXXI 1967, 125-6.

F443 see F450 for new edition.

F533 for ARTHURI read ARTHURIAN.

G11 for SEE #5258 read SEE O61.

G35 for BBSIA/1977 read BBSIA/XXIX.

G68 after author's name add ED.

G172 delete CF. BBSIA, XXIV 1972, 335.

G205 for POIRUS read PORIUS.

G263 delete penultimate review.

H66 for BBSIA/XVII read BBSIA/XVIII.

H129 this is an edition.

H133 add ET after PERCEVAL.

H303 see also K143 and N68.

H360 after author's name add ED.

H398 after author's name add ED.

H499 for NYME read NYMUE.

H601 for LANGESZELET". MELAN POUR read LANZELET·.
          MELANGES POUR.

H607 after author's name add ED.

H637 insert H637 before "TRADITION AND ORIGINALITY.

H660 at end of entry add SEE ALSO WHITTEREDGE, GWENETH.

J77 add 4. AUFLAGE, 1973. SUMMARY IN BBSIA, XXVII, 129.

J111 delete whole item - it is J92.

J164 add JOHNSON, F.C., ED.

J193 for ANTIQUITY, 80 read ANTIQUITY, XX.

J295 after title add MA, LVIII 1952, 281-298.

K16 for KAKURAI, ITO, TRANS. read KAKURAI, SHUKUSHI, ET AL., TRANS

K22, K23 for KALUZA, MAY read KALUZA, MAX.

K126 for NOTES OF read NOTES ON.

K139 for CARIO read CAIRO.

K143 see also H303

K194 for KITTEREDGE read KITTREDGE.

K197 for KITTERIDGE read KITTREDGE.

K446 for ITEM #2999 read K438.

L115 after COURTESY add ESSAYS IN MEMORY OF C.S. LEWIS.

L150 line 5 should read DU MS.B.N.FR. 794.

L197 for UNIV. OF MO. read UNIV. OF MISSOURI.

L359 delete first IN.

L468 line 8 for JEGCPH read JEGP.

L571 see also L565 and L566.

L625 should read "L'YSTORIA TRISTAN ET LA QUESTION DES
     ARCHETYPES". REVUE CELTIQUE, XXIV 1913, 41FF.

L666 before 410 insert DIED.

M97 also entered as N68, see also H303.

M222-M225 see also MOISES, MASSAUD.

M361 add review BY G. DI STEFANO IN SF, XLI 1970, P. 323.

M483 after author's name add ED. For LES read LAIS.

M600-M601 see also MASSAUD, MOISES.

M656 after author's name add ED.

M685 add REPRINTED IN MORTON, A.L. "THE MATTER OF

BRITAIN, ESSAYS IN A LIVING CULTURE", LONDON:
LAWRENCE AND WISHART, 1966, 9-35.

N68 also entered as M97, see also H303.

N89 after BIRTHPLACE add (J130).

p. 539 add NORMAN, FREDERICK, ED.
        N262A   [BBSIA/XX/99]
        "ESSAYS IN GERMAN LITERATURE, I", LONDON:
        UNIVERSITY OF LONDON, INSTITUTE OF GERMANIC
        STUDIES, 1965.
        REVIEWS, ETC.: BY GORDON L. TRACY IN MONATS.,
        LIX 1967, 371-2.

P17 for PAGAES, AMADEU read PAGES, AMADEU.

P49 after authors' names add EDS.

P286 after LANCAROTE add VOL. I TEXTS, VOL. II COMMENTARY.

R132 for CAMPION read CHAMPION.

R139 after author's name add ED.

p. 622 add RODRIGUEZ DE MONTALVO, GARCIA, ED.
        R381A   [BBSIA/XXII/131]
        "AMADIS DE GAULA". CON UN ESTUDIO PRELIMINAR,
        BIBLIOGRAFIA SELECCIONADA E INDICE DE NOMBRES
        PROPIOS POR DA. ANGELES CARDONA DE GILBERT ...
        Y D. JOAQUIN RAFAEL FONTANALS, BARCELONA: ED.
        BRUGUERA, 1969 (LIBRO CLASICO, VOL. 21).

R400 see also C297.

R416 this is an edition.

S105 delete last line.

p. 647 add S105A   [MLQ/1953/3681]
        "Some Observations on King Arthur", OC, V 1951,
        43-44.

S254 delete CF. BBSIA, XXI, 1969, 174.

S457 see also B924 BURKE SEVERS, J.

S474 for MALORY read MALORY (KAY, BEDIVERE, PELLES).

S623 this is an edition.

S628 this is an edition.

S689 for #5110 read S685.

S864 for MELANGES F. LECOY read MLG (MELANGES LE GENTIL).

S914 delete second review.

T167 for BBSIA/XIX/214 read BBSIA/XIX/215.

p. 737 TRAYNIER, JEAN, see CHAMPION, PIERRE, C147.

V79 add review BY B. FOLKART IN SF, LVI 1975, p. 322.

W40 after author's name add ED.

W97 for BBSIA/XVIII/34 read BBSIA/XVIII/35.

W236 for MLQ/1950/3923 read MLQ/1950/3293.

W426 for WILLIAMS, MARY read WILLIAMS, MARY RHIANNON.

W436 for MELANGES read STUDIES.

W509 after author's name add ED.

p. 802 under WOLEDGE, BRIAN, ED. add W582A L'ATRE PERILLEUX,
          CLASSIQUES FRANCAIS DU MOYEN AGE, NO. 76, PARIS:
          CHAMPION, 1936.

W639-W640 after author's name add ED.

Z86 REVIEWS, antepenultimate line, delete OF 2ND. ED.

Z89 for #3179B read W45.

                          NOTES

ARTHURIAN LITERATURE IN THE MIDDLE AGES #4737 is to be
found at L575.

MMEV is to be found at M551.

Not all volumes of Studies, Melanges, Festschriften etc. have
substantive entries in the author listing, since they are not
all listed separately in our sources. See under "Festschriften"
in the index for details of the item numbers of such volumes
and the articles appearing in them. In the
process of up-dating the bibliography we shall endeavour to
list separately all composite volumes of Arthurian studies
and their contents.

'Aaque Aquee' A133.
'Ab Lo Pascor' D91.
Abbey, E. A. B800.
Abbrevia_io G106.
Abductions W164.
Abelard W655.
Abelardian Ethics H645.
Abella S101.
'Abenteuerbuch'. See Ulrich Fueetrer.
'Aber' in Gottfried's 'Tristan' C425.
Accalon W49.
'Achilleid' C358.
Acrostic (Tristan) F287.
'Adam, Le Jeu d'' L710.
Adaptations B948, D18, F300, H597, H599, H600, H605, K87.
Adonis W260.
Adultery G436, H645, L242, T5.
Adventure B339A, B405, B728, F155, G304, H226, K338, T135,
Z58.
Aedhan Mac Gabhrain J81, P69.
Aelle W26.
Aeneas A238, C343, D27, G271, S26, T43.
See also 'Eneas'.
Aeneas and Lavinia Love Story W573.
Aeneas-Dido Allusion in Chretien's 'Erec et Enide' W573.
'Aeneid'. See Heinrich van Veldeken, and Virgil.
Aesthetic Criticism A58, H217.
Aesthetic Distance in Chretien G364.
Aesthetics B156, B463, B538, B720, B858, C447, F149, F478,
G170, H173, J329, K302, L253, L450, R70, S135, S214, S266, W41,
W194, W516, Z79.
Aetius J192.
'Afallennau' C221, J100.
Agaeles Thrap A239.
Agape B34.
Agned, Mons B421.
'Agravain' M466.
Ailred of Rievaulx L187.
'Aiol' M357.
Alain de Gomeret B841.
Alain of Lille, 'De Planctu Naturae' L698, L699.
Alan of Galloway G313.
Alban, Saint C398, L283.
Albany J27.
Alberic de Pisancon, 'Alexandre' H266.
'Alberic, Vision de' M125.
Albigenses B637, B688.
Albigensians R24, R25.
Albion J13, S348.
Albrecht IV M3.
Albrecht von Scharfenberg H46, L137, M257, W617.
  'Der Juengere Titurel' A83, B180, B448, B568, B907, B908,

<1>

E55, F285, G202, G364, G388, H343, H595, H653, H654, J65, K152, K271, K339, L135, L136, L137, L263, M3, M167, M408, M704, O37, R19, R244, R245, R385, R453, R468, S394, T136, T250, T252, V112, W607, W609, W611, W612, W614, W615, W616, W61., W618, W619, Z19, Z20.

Alchemy D317, O8, T50.

Aldingar, Sir C198A.

Alexander H203, H253, I20, L86.

'Alexanderlied' G307.

'Alexandre, Libro de' C59, C62, L724, M479.

'Alexandre L'Orphelin' B490, B503, P268, W259.

Alexis le Protosebastos C60.

Alfred, King A40.

'Alis and the Problem of Time in 'Cliges'' N233.

'Aliscans' L392.

All Saints' Day R39.

Allegory   B281, B332, C148, C229, E123, F415, H323, J38, J50, J203, K212, L460, M287, M554, M558, M593, O35, P277, R59, R72, R196, R323, S498, T283, W287, W288.

Alliterative Poetry D291, H370, H628, L195, L448, L697, O2, O3, R486, S258, S468, S947, T277, W59.

Alliterative Revival S22, S23.

Alliterative Romances B138, D7, D143, L566, O58.

Alliterative Song M238.

Almain B850.

Alphonso X K8, M371.

Alphonso XI M370.

Alsace P392.

'Altromh Tigh' D200, D296.

'Amadace, Sir' B766, D148.

Amadeus, VI, Count of Savoy A237.

'Amadis' G145, M83, M727, O56, P6, P307, P308, P310, R375, V1.

'Amadis de Gaula' A137, A288, B555, C90, C356, F158, F497, H243, J61, J62, L76, L78, L79, L131, L584, M160, M176, M179, M246, M481, M513, M695, P280, P294, P309, P311, P312, R381A, R382, R383, R448, S9, S417, S620, T98, T240, W159, W175, W375.

'Amadis et Ydoine' J116, L2, L718, R132, R133.

'Amadis of Greece' L123.

Amalrich von Bena G183.

Ambiguous Oath B59.

'Ambraser Heldenbuch' J66, U12.

Ambrosius Aurelius A264, B227, B901, C121, C391, C393, D121, F212, H134, J85, K114, L309, M274, S11.

American Literature B961, B962, M309, S776.
See also individual authors.

Amfreville-sous-les-Monts L720.

'Amis et Amile' B56, G187.

'Amis and Amiloun' H543.

'Amisties de Vraie Amour' T100.

<2>

'Amlyn ac Amic' G187.
Amlawd Wledig J85.
'Amorosa Visione' B355, B651, B652.
Amour Courtois. See Courtly Love.
Amphibalus, Saint F29, T22.
Amplificatio G106.
Amytans Episode S146.
Anaphora W573.
'Ancren Riwle' A122, E166.
Andreas Capellanus   B116,   B275,   B276,   B591,   B652,   C142,
D125, D126, D127, E82, F224, F325, G155, J31, J36, K185, M68,
M316, N294, P92, R358, S198, S199, S236, S494, S796, T29, T235,
V89, W198, Z88.
   'De Amore' B922, F352, J33, P17, P18, S64, S917, T257, Z11.
   'De Arte Honeste Amandi' F351, K192.
Andret B733.
Andronique C60.
Aneirin or Aneurin, 'Gododdin'   B63, B757, C396, H83, H357,
J7, J15, J18, J26, J265, J282, L344, M662, P100, W20, W379,
W404, W407.
'Aneurin, Book of' G324.
Anfortas   A120, B375,   D93, E67, G376, H173, H393, J173,
S629, T207.
Angels W472.
Angles L605.
Anglesey J276, W422.
Anglicus Caudatus, 'Englishmen with Tails' L56.
Anglo-Latin K50.
Anglo-Norman Literature B690, L183, M485, W58, W242.
Anglo-Norman Studies S513.
Anglo-Normans R502.
'Anglo-Saxon Chronicle' B237, B723, D135, H624.
Anglo-Saxon Conquest R103.
Anglo-Saxon Invasion D24, R94.
Anglo-Saxon Writers S267.
Anglo-Saxons B415, C228, H408, W5.
Anguinguerren L148.
Animals in Arthurian Literature J112, L316.
See also Bestiaries.
Anjou S173, S591.
'Annales Cambriae'   B757, C123, F26, G1, G2, H622, J282,
L566, L570, L635, R206, R537, W15, W34, W131.
'Annals of Inisfallen' M6.
Annanchet M728.
'Annolied' P236.
Annwn L521, R489.
'Anonymous Riming Chronicle' C72, Z39.
'Antapodosis, L'' M328.
Anthologies A209, C274, G382, H331, J201, J310, L582, M212,
M653, M691, N88, P199, R279, W77, Z73.
Anthropology L279.

<3>

<4>

L377, L459, M130, M277, M732, N70, O53, P23, P36, P37, P39,
P221, P305, P359, P389, P391, R33, R48, R399, R461, S55, S341,
S449, T59, T272, V2, W681, Z66, Z77, Z78, Z81, Z82, Z84, Z85.
Arithmetic in Medieval Poetry E30.
Arlette B643.
'armiu wip' B605.
Arms and Armour A12, B665, W232.
Arms, Coats of. See Heraldry.
Arnaut Daniel O51.
Arnive (King Arthur's Mother) H625.
Arnold, Matthew, 'Tristram and Iseult' B122, B141, B749,
C217, C359, H577, R121, R414, S858, W620.
Art C237, D316, F534, H169, H218, H294, K218, L579, O116,
O117, R96, S147.
See also Iconography, and Modena Sculpture.
Artemis S759.
'Arthour and Merlin' F473, H511, K299, L360, L376, M38,
M44, M45, M318, S548, S549, S550, S584, W72.
Arthur A17, A102, A104, A118, A121, A175, A176, A177, A186,
A192, A199, A214, A215, A223, A225, A226, A262, A263, A264,
A265, A268, A274, B29, B62, B63, B64, B103, B256, B271, B340,
B364, B383, B400, B406, B409, B410, B412, B544, B578, B689,
B723, B728, B757, B789, B798, B813, B868, C1, C77, C113, C118,
C128, C137, C141, C171, C208, C290, C291, C327, C334, C351,
C391, C395, C416, C419, C438, D2, D23, D36, D88, D89, D93,
D150, D152, D174, D206, D227, D237, D298, E23, E80, E162, F24,
F25, F79, F121, F133, F307, F482, F483, F530, G15, G33, G97,
G98, G131, G140, G164, G165, G178, G179, G180, G247, G275,
G278, G285, G340, G349, G376, G428, G455, H18, H72, H92, H125,
H134, H161, H225, H322, H341, H353, H385, H400, H405, H413,
H414, H506, H509, H542, H549, H610, H623, H655, H667, I5, I20,
I27, J11, J14, J18, J22, J23, J57, J81, J87, J128, J145, J153,
J195, J199, J206, J208, J274, J275, J284, J285, K91, K92, K103,
K104, K106, K114, K121, K124, K127, K134, K217, K218, K266,
K280, K313, K390, L19, L57, L58, L59, L60, L61, L62, L70, L81,
L87, L126, L244, L280, L375, L407, L415, L451, L464, L470,
L496, L502, L522, L532, L559, L566, L630, L636, L669, L684,
L685, L692, L700, M91, M92, M146, M209, M305, M430, M511, M516,
M570, M610, M635, M680, M718, M721, M733, M739, N60, N89, N124,
N159, N161, N164, N182, N188, N205, N234, N265, O94, O114, P57,
P68, P69, P72, P105, P287, P405, R8, R14, R16, R17, R101, R121,
R220, R275, R304, R353, R369, R396, R506, R524, R537, S11,
S102, S105A,S113, S114, S146, S186, S203, S210, S411, S413, S433,
S452, S462, S477, S520, S569, S571, S645, S674, S704, S776,
S810, S812, S814, S839, S943, T69, T109, T217, T226, T247,
T283, U14, V32, V84, W25, W33, W51, W52, W70, W137, W193, W220,
W252, W273, W282, W372, W395, W424, W434, W441, W477, W529,
W659, W674.
'Arthur' (English Medieval Poem) F128.
'Arthur' (Turkish translation) A274.
'Arthur and Gorlagon' B265, K197, K351, K369, K375, M93.
'Arthur and Lucius' D45, D145, M171, S898, W668, W669,

<5>

W671.

Arthur d'Algarve R247.

'Arthur of Little Britain', '(Petit) Artus de Bretagne' C202, C285, C378, L143, L158, L656, M487, M560, O9, S175, S188, S720, S721, S722, W577, W653.

'King Arthur and King Cornwall' D47, K375, R134, W73.

'King Arthur and King Mark' K121.

'King Arthur's Death' (Ballad) W532.

Arthur, Historical C292.

Arthur, Prince B257.

Arthur, Saint M227

Arthur's Battles. See Battles, Arthur's.

'Arthur's Britain' A111, A267.

'Arthur's Colloquy with the Eagle' W424.

Arthur's Death B274, B817, B896, C3, C419, E153, G356, L470, M522, M719, S461, V85, Z15.

Arthur's Dream. S645.

Arthur's Grave and Burial B896, E153, G356, L415, M719, V85.

Arthur's Hall. See Tintagel.

Arthur's 'Kinging' G408.

Arthur's Lance. See Ron.

Arthur's Mantle E147, T95.

Arthur's Northern Conquests M718.

'Arthur's O'On' B799.

Arthur's Origin U8.

Arthur's Rescue K123.

Arthur's Return T273, W144, W329, W530.

Arthur's Shield H405, P258, P279.

Arthur's Stone H310.

Arthur's Survival B773, S114.

See also Dryden, John.

Arthur's Sword. See Excalibur.

'Arthur's Tomb' L126, R8, T287.

Arthurian Battlefields. See Badon Hill, and Battlefields, Arthurian.

Arthurian Bibliography B802, B804, B805, B806, B807, B808, C155, H14, H15, H16, H17, K436, K437, L325, M28, M30, N33, N34, N35, N36, N37, N168, N169, N170, P86, P87, P90, P95, P224, P225, R252, S108, S210, S601, S602, S603, S604, S605, S606, S607, S608, S609, S610, S614, S615, S616, V88, W216, W592, Z95.

See also Bibliographies.

Arthurian Campaign E157.

Arthurian Characters F286.

Arthurian Chronicles M221.

Arthurian Comedy E10, E11.

Arthurian Compilations H376.

Arthurian Congress A178, A189, A190, A208, A212, C316, D236, F1, F389, F446, G10, H75, L171, L367, L529, M200, P150, R153, S448, W120, W122, W540.

Arthurian Court B35, G96, P326, W676.

<6>

Arthurian Criticism H578.
Arthurian Cult B114, J198.
Arthurian Cycle R114, W276.
Arthurian Epitaphs C295.
Arthurian Feast S142.
Arthurian Geography B840, B843.
Arthurian Heraldry B663, B664.
Arthurian Heroes B597.
Arthurian Influences L555, V97, V101.
Arthurian Legend A108, B33, B64, B311, B318, B436, B727,
B746, B856, B896, C132, D88, D115, E110, F28, F64, F223, G397,
H148, I4, J121, J179, J208, J246, J274, J282, L71, L244, L504,
L523, L525, L548, L554, L559, L561, L566, L570, L636, M29, M71,
M187, M190, M403, M404, N147, N174, P223, P304, R184, R308,
R370, S362, S433, S537, S556, S776, S777, S865, T184, T271,
V64, V102, W318, W366.
Arthurian Literature A194, B62, B76, B256, B767, F453, G17,
G180, H148, H149, H183, H316, J245, J280, L179, L326, L566,
L575, M207, N150, O109, P116, P263, R180, S440, T274, T286,
U16, U17, U19, W584.
Arthurian Names. See Names.
Arthurian Newsletter N136, N138, S94.
Arthurian Notes N123.
Arthurian Origins B33, B311, B436, B856, D115, F28, L504,
L572, L636, R370, S556, V102.
Arthurian Pageant O41.
Arthurian Pedigree T193.
Arthurian Problems N213.
Arthurian Prologues H635.
Arthurian Relics D177.
Arthurian Romance A51, A115, B68, B69, B78, B115, B367,
B433, B446, B476, B617, B829, D106, E9, E117, F123, F223, F253,
F353, F462, G17, G31, G215, G236, H141, H490, H523, H619, I34,
J36, J292, K254, K258, K259, K377, L180, L280, L513, L514,
L518, L519, L579, L668, L699, M196, M548, N31, N32, N67, N228,
O108, P16, P47, P50, P82, P146, P256, P260, P261, P390, P407,
R121, R174, R253, R263, S153, S167, S182, S337, S630, S632,
S681, S682, S824, S829, T124, V106, W52, W220, W248, W252,
W275, W319, W385, W447, W483, W534, Y18, Z73.
See also Matter of Britain and individual authors and
countries.
Arthurian Scholars N140.
Arthurian Sites B558, E72, J21, R9.
See also Archaeology, and Battlefields, Arthurian.
Arthurian Society D240, F445, F448, F456, J151, S536, W122.
Arthurian Studies B727, L568.
Arthurian Texts C85.
'Arthurian Torso' W365.
Arthurian Tradition J276, L552, L560, P168.
See also Matter of Britain.
Arthuriana B100, B558, B816, B822, H468, K435, L37, N187,

<7>

N196, W371.
Arthurians, List of A28, F446, F458, N154.
Arts of Love B4, F104, L142.
'Artur Moi Mac Ri I N-Eivinn' M31.
'Artus de Bretagne, Petit'. See 'Arthur of Little Britain'.
Arveragus A236, C378, L143.
Arwirac of Glastonbury W319.
'Asclepios' K7.
'Aspremont' B550, F220.
'Assertion of King Arthure'. See Leland, John, 'Assertio
Inclytissimi Arthuri'.
'Astolat, The Fair Maid of' V85.
Astrology K161, R245, V32.
Athanasian Creed T207.
Athelstan C290, L480, L481, R445, Y11.
Atlantis B650.
'Atre Perilleux' B152, H503, K362, O21, P164, S162, W117,
W576, Z69.
'Auberon' W385.
'Aucassin et Nicolette' G433, M329, W367.
'Aude et Yseut devant la Mort' S925.
Audelay, John, 'Poems' W328.
'Audigier' S514.
Auerbach, Erich B170, J330, V34.
Augustin, Saint S305.
Augustinian Love-Theory M178.
Aurelius Ambrosius. See Ambrosius Aurelius.
Austrian Ballads L114, T130.
Automata B814.
Avalon, Avallach A220, A262, B543, B650, B896, C55, C162,
C163, C188, C320, F22, F347, G135, G349, H155, J145, K334,
K386, L496, L516, L594, M470, S101, S557, S828, T190, T217,
W114, W329.
'Avarchide' F414.
Avenable T143.
Averroism D126.
Avicenna F5, G404.
'Avowing of King Arthur' B766, D6, D7, D148, F474, I27,
S808, T189.
'Awntyrs of(f) Arthure' A157, B608, B706, B940, C195, D148,
G68, G69, H129, H130, H131, H344, H539, H547, H548, I27, K198,
P120, S808, T276, T277.

<8>

'Bacheler' F175.
Badda B810.
Baddon R206.
Badon Hill   B723, B927, D202, J21, J188, J191, R103, S11,
S943, W26.
Battlefields, Arthurian. See also Battle of Mount Badon; Battles;
Battles, Arthur's.
'Bahrprobe' B345.
'Baile et Ailinn' M100.
Baillods, Edouard B205.
'Baladro del Sabio Merlin'   B485, B529, B554, M209, M640,
M641, P276.
See also Merlin.
'Balain' C27, L188, M201, M208, V41, V65.
Balar ua Neid O15.
Balin B775, R212.
See also Balain and Malory.
'Ballad of King Arthur' M522, W452.
'Ballad of King Arthur and King Cornwall' W73.
Ballads   B276, B760, C173, C198A, F460, F489, G276, H585,
L127, T279.
Balor with the Evil Eye K351.
Baltic Towns S186.
Ban of Benuich T150.
Bandello K46.
Bangor Iscoed L405.
Barbarossa W293.
Bardic Tradition A52.
Bards R502.
See also Welsh Bards.
Barenton, Fountain of D195, F265, M537.
'Barlaam et Josaphat' L109.
'Barzaz-Breiz'. See Hersart de la Villemarque.
'Basingwerk, Book of' G353, G355.
'Batard de Bouillon (Le)' C321.
Bath C410.
'Bataille de Caresme et de Charnage' L655.
'Bataille Loquifer' T217, W127.
Battle of Arthuret P1.
Battle of Borguion J14.
Battle of Hastings C210.
Battle of Mag Tuired or Magh Tuireadh H87, O13, O14.
Battle of Mount Badon B376, G350, S817.
Battle of Moytura S713.
Battle of Salisbury M280.
Battlefields, Arthurian B723, S822, T225.
See also Badon Hill.
Battles B885, B927, C291, H651, N205, W400.
Battles, Arthur's A268, B376, C393, C395, D192, E187, J11,
J186, R104, W294.
Baudemaguz L515, S29.
'Bauduins Butors' T147, T148, T149, T150.

<9>

Baugh, Albert Croll L128.
Beardsley, Aubrey F121, W67.
Beau Couart. See Coward, Handsome.
'Beaudous' G241.
Beaumains G297, G417, L520.
'Beaurepaire' C60, F293, J158.
See also Castles.
Becfhola D160.
Becket, Thomas C162, C367, G15.
Beddau Stanzas J284.
Bede A154, B224, B415, D115, H624, M577.
Bedier, Joseph C85, C457, N193, P244, R428, V68.
 'Tristan' B209, S69, S570, S633, V39.
Bedivere G285, S474.
Beer Test R69.
Bek, Thomas, of Castleford, 'Chronicle' B224, B225.
Belakane W463.
Belgian Literature C160, P313.
Belin and Brenne B428.
'Bel Inconnu'. See Fair Unknown and Renaud de Beaujeau.
Bellezza Corre G424.
Bellicart G285.
Bellow, Saul, 'Henderson The Rain King' L124.
Bendigeidfran L336.
See also Bran the Blessed.
Benoist Rigaud P265.
Benoit de Sainte Maure L677, S515.
Beot E47.
'Beowulf' R269, Z38.
Bercilak C143, C439, E1, H166, H335, J45, S466, T4, T77,
T85.
Bercilak (Lady) S38.
Bercilak de Haut Desert S587.
'Berinus' S722.
Bernard, Saint, of Clairvaux B360, G279, S236, W472, W473.
Berne. See 'Folie Tristan'.
Berners, Lord. See Bouchier, John.
Bernhard de Ventadour D70, D86.
Berni, Francesco C175, D279, M19, P358, S634.
Bernward, Saint M420.
Beroul A43, A161, A285, B59, B73, B164, B201, B236, B343,
B646, C20, C95, C96, C344, D64, D65, D182, E182, F494, G427,
H330, H458, H502, J115, J165, J294, J304, J307, J318, L39,
L165, L166, L169, L178, L228, L722, M347, M354, P20, P165,
R150, R373, R418, S917, S944, T6, T8, V4, V79, W308, W369,
W541, W580.
 'Tristan' B59, B73, B80, B260, B330, B354, B395, B396,
B397, B438, B644, B645, B733, C94, C97, C196, C197, C417, D65,
D82, D87, D112, E141, E183, F59, F60, F71, F262, F404, F406,
F407, F433, G130, G148, G363, H13, H139, H330, H332, H333,
H334, H415, H502, H645, H647, J69, J71, J156, J297, J298, J302,

<10>

J303, L22, L138, L146, L148, L167, L185, L242, L426, L447,
M186, M191, M353, M417, M574, M599, M736, M737, N156, N157,
N232, P164, P314, R80, R81, R82, R84, R85, R86, R122, R123,
R124, R125, R126, R268, R372, R511, S779, S887, S888, S926,
V19, V23, V53, V68, V71, V74, W52, W302, W330, W331, Y13.
  Corrections to edition of 'Tristan' D64.
Bertilak. See Bercilak.
Bertran de Born L161.
Besieged Ladies N134.
Beste Glatissante. See Questing Beast.
Bestiaries C439, J112, L186, S695.
Bethides F187.
Beverus, Johannes H103.
'Beuve de Hanstone' B184.
'Bevys of Hampton' B138, V11.
'Biausdous, Roman de' L33.
Bible D111, F100, H112, S32.
'Bible Moralisee' S892.
Biblical Elements L193, W280.
Biblical Influences F309.
Bibliographies A29, A30, A31, A34, A35, A36, A37, A38, A50,
A92, A217, A218, A272, A275, B38, B115, B347, B348, B453, B524,
B525, B527, B528, B558, B596, B801, B802, B803, B804, B805,
B806, B807, B808, B809, B871, B922, B939, C155, C404, C405,
C406, C407, C408, D140, D234, D255, D256, D258, D260, D261,
D262, D263, D316, F12, F16, F38, F159, F269, F270, F271, F273,
F274, F275, F276, F277, F446, F447, F449, F451, F452, F458,
F487, F519, F520, G280, G320, G331, G384, H14, H15, H16, H17,
H141, H148, H159, H181, H491, H523, J292, J318, K79, K80, K89,
K102, K175, K176, K177, K304, K331, K421, K434, K435, K437,
L19, L54, L325, L387, L449, L518, L673, L674, L675, M28, M29,
M30, M78, M104, M144, M310, M440, M672, M733, N30, N32, N33,
N34, N35, N36, N37, N136, N140, N153, N168, N169, N170, N266,
O65, P74, P75, P76, P77, P78, P79, P80, P81, P82, P83, P84,
P85, P86, P88, P89, P90, P93, P96, P223, P224, P274, P293,
P400, R121, R135, R161, R163, R164, R165, R166, R167, R252,
R315, R316, R317, R382, R383, R412, R413, R552, R553, R554,
S210, S242, S483, S606, S611, S612, S613, T129, T130, T154,
T156, T157, T158, T159, T160, T221, U19, V35, W216, W222, W371,
W562, W563, W564, W585, W590, W593, W646, Z95.
See also Arthurian Bibliography.
  Anglo-Saxon B558.
  Austrian A218, F16, G384, K89.
  Belgian F270, R161, R162, R163, R164, R165, R166, R167.
  Brazilian B526, B527, B528.
  Breton P333.
  British B115, H180, H579, H580, M28, M30, N168, N169, N170,
P224, P225, S108, T154, T155, T156, T157, T158, T159, T160,
T201, T202, T203.
  Canadian A32, A34, A35, A36, A37, A38.
  Celtic B347, B348, B558, C155, F487, L325, N32, N34, N35,

<11>

N36, N37, W216.
 Danish L672, L673, L674, L675.
 Dutch D234, D255, D256, D257, D258, D260, D261, D262, D263.
 French   B594,   B596, F269, F270, F271, F272, F273, F274,
F275, F276, F277, H14, H15, H16, H17, H534, K437, M607, R252,
W583, W584, W586, W587, W588, W589, W590, W591, W592, W593.
 German A218, D140, F16, F519, F520, G384, H180, H181, K76,
K80, K89, K175, K176, K177, M78, O65, R223, S210, S311, S738,
W562, W563, W564.
 Irish F11, F12.
 Italian C404, C405, C406, C407, C408, C453, V105.
 Middle English T198, T199, T200, T201, T202, T203, U18.
 Portuguese B524, B525, B526, B527, B528.
 Spanish B524, B525, B526, B527, B528.
 Swedish R411, R412, R413.
 Swiss R551, R552, R553, R554.
 Turkish A275.
 U.S.A. A30, A31, A32, A34, A35, A36, A37, A38.
 Welsh N33, N37, P101, T155.
'Bibliotheca Arnamagnaenna' S192.
'Bibliotheca Celtica' B349, J243.
'Bibliotheque Bleue' M105, M672.
Bilis D87.
Bipartite Composition of Romances H220, H583.
Bird Tree in 'Yvain' M328.
'Bisclaveret'. See Marie de France.
'Black   Book   of Carmarthen'   J80, J97, J100, J104, J105,
J284, L324, L404, L410, R206.
Black Chapel N234.
Black Prince F135.
Blackmore, Sir Richard R443.
Bladud F23.
Blake, William F514, W141.
'Blancandrin et L'Orgueilleuse d'Amours' S649, S650.
'Blanchandrain' F299.
Blancheflor-Perceval Question C60, H64, K213, N139, N218.
Blanchette F189.
'Blandin of Cornwall' B931, C21, H571, W47.
Blanscheflur C219, W596.
See also Blancheflor-Perceval Question and 'Floire et Blancheflor'.
Blathnat T280.
'Blazon, Early' B667.
Bleddri. See Breri.
Bledhericus. See Breri.
Bleeding Lance. See Lance, Bleeding.
Blegobred L637.
'Blegywyrd' (Book of) E84.
Bleheri-Bledri. See Breri.
Bleheri, Bleheris. See Breri.
Blennerhasset, Thomas C28.
'Bleu Chevalier, Le' C81.
Bleys G285.

<12>

Bligger von Steinach K311.
Bliocadran B848, S781, W639, W640.
'Bliocadran Prologue' T120, W247.
Blood Drops on the Snow G188, G359, K283, P339.
Blood Mystique R444.
Blysse and Blunder in 'Sir Gawain and the Green Knight'
T52.
Boar, The Mouth of the T84.
Boccaccio B355, B651, B652, B824, L677.
  'Decameron' G231.
Boethius, 'De Consolatione Philosophiae' L685.
Bogomils S203.
Boiardo B258, B353, C33, C42, C109, F207, G342, G343, R118,
S112, S441, W358.
  'Orlando Innamorato' A256, C174, D279, G136, P35, P36, P40,
P370, P406, R38, R539, S112, S690, T217, W681, Z80, Z83, Z85.
'Boivre Amoureux, Le' M75.
'Bonedd yr Arwyr' B96, B98.
Boniface of Montferrat L458.
'Book of Basingwerk' W393.
Bors L683.
Boun de Hamtone W133.
Bourchier, John, Lord Berners M560, O9.
Boutiere, Jean C247.
'Boy and the Mantle, The' T94.
'Boy's King Arthur, Boy's Mabinogion, Boy's Froissart' L70.
Brabon Silvius, Brabantian Swanknight B443.
Brain Mac Febail B319.
'Brait, Conte del' B485, B554, B628, P276.
'Bran Galed' J232.
Bran the Blessed K379, K382, K390, L344, L347, L506, L540,
L548, L581, M138, N129, N130, N131, N286, P71, S508.
Brangaene J30, J50, W250.
Brangien F8, R65, S722.
'Branwen' (Mabinogi of) H239, J230, J231, J281, L336, M13,
M14, M15, M18, R489, T131, W48.
'Braull' L567.
Brendan, Saint (Voyage of) A265, B237, B246, D244, D247,
D254, D280, H220, L183, L186, M125, M328, P22, R482, S442,
S443, W118, W119.
'Brenhinedd y Saesson' J286.
Brent Knoll D202.
Breri B846, B894, G17, H165, K86, L337, L491, L495, L598,
O109A, W258, W432.
'Bret' J164.
See also Brait.
'Breta Soegur' L432, T218.
Breton A4, A5, A6, A7, A163, B233, B842, D181, H308, L134,
L566, L653, P287, V100.
Breton Character S900, S901.
Breton Cycle V27.

<13>

Breton Folklore D184, L534.
Breton History R98, W101.
Breton Hope B364.
Breton Lais B1, B115, B740, B745, B747, B898, D51, D116, D214, D216, F238, F241, H431, H442, L479, P181, P218, R525, S190, S544, S586, W387.
Breton Language G252.
Breton Legal Institutions S900.
Breton Legends A277, C165, J136, L81, L258.
Breton Literature F254, F372, F378, G252, H570, J179, L63, L722, P333.
Breton Oral Tradition L652, S75.
Breton Romances G431, G434, H568.
Breton Saints C361, D195, D199, H165.
Breton Sources F289. Z53A,
Breton Versions H309, L257, S375.
Bretons L605.
Bretwalda C126.
'Breuddwyd Maxen'. See 'Maxen, Dream of'.
Brian des Illes W269.
Brieuc, Saint C362.
Brigid, Saint R371.
Bristol Channel C55.
Britain B259, C132, D186, L184, R251, V93, W372, W658.
Britain, Early B386, B623, C159, E43, H134, J18, N28.
Britain, Legendary History T33.
Britain, Roman R537, W23.
Britanni V25.
British Church C123, C124, C133.
British History C112, C113, C114, C116, C119, C120, C334, J17, L375.
'Brito di Brettagna' F256, S56.
Britons, Origins of C261, W5.
Brittany A238, B842, C5, C129, C130, D194, D312, F256, F258, J179, L122, L285, M142, M144, M145, M147, M156, M537, R483, S555.
Brityna K92.
Broceliande C130, C221, C267, C268, D315, F265, F268, G151, H94, H669, L192, L258, M135, M469, R115, S27, S779, T150, W377.
Brochefort, The Hermit of the Forest of T150.
Bron L501, M470, N181.
Brother Robert H53, T218.
  'Tristrams Saga' B879, H52, H53, H54, H165, H385, K297, K298, L125, S118, S119, S120, S121, S122, S123, S124, S125, S126, S127, T254, Y9, Y11.
Brown, A. C. L. W307.
Browning, Robert, 'Childe Roland' A244, L371.
Bruce, J. D. L542, W383.
'Brun de la Montaigne' J71, M428.
Brun von Schoenbeck W621.
Brunel, Clovis V35.

<14>

'Brut' or 'Chronicle of England' A213, A254, B233, B643, C187, G353, G355, H103, H169, K313, L189, L321, L355, L403, M361, P91, P384, R459, S150, S502, S775, W20, Z18.
See also Layamon, Lawman, and Wace.
'Brut' (Alderman) R109.
'Brut, An Anglo-Norman' B241.
'Brut' (English) L113, Z39.
'Brut Gruffud ab Arthur' R333.
'Brut' (Harley) B393, B394.
'Brut' (Munich) H474.
'Brut' (Royal) B235.
'Brut y Brenhinedd' J99, J260, L319, P91, R144, R332.
'Brut Tysilio' F512, J88, L314, L355, M1, R333, R334, S363, S646, Z18.
'Brut y Tywysogion' J288, J289, T8.
Brutes Albyon S582.
'Bruts' (Welsh) B856, E84, F512, J222, L318, L319, L320, L322, L638, M1, P66, P91, R341, R342, W20.
Brutus A238, D271, F512, G131, G132, H169, M1, M62, M667, S205, S497, W9.
Brutus Legend H188.
Brychan H663, T110.
Buchet O80.
Buddhism E15.
'Buile Suibhne' J5, L196, O44.
Bulgarian Influence T117.
Burials E151.
Burne-Jones J215.
Burning at the Stake R137.
Byzantine Sources V96, V99.
Byzantium S456.

<15>

Cabala A73.
'Caballero Zifar' A119, D314, M729, S417, S783.
Cadbury Castle Excavations A104, A105, A106, A107, A113,
A114, A267.
See also Archaeology, Camelot, and Castles.
Cadoc, Saint G370, W140.
See also 'Vita Cadoci'.
Cador K313.
Cadwalader B624, G131.
Cadwy fab Geraint R203.
Caen C316.
Caergai R353.
Caerleon C55, D88, F412, N28, N29, S843, S868, W285, Y11.
Caerleon-on-Usk B763.
Caernarvonshire G338.
Caerwent N29.
Caesar, Julius L21, N63, N64.
Cai fab Cynyr J251.
Calderon F34.
Caldey W32.
Caledfwlch L345.
Calendars L162, L241, S480.
Caliburn L643.
Calidon C221.
See also Battles, Arthur's.
Caledonian Forest C221.
See also Forests.
Caloain M742.
Calogrenant, Calogrenanz H635, L463, L500, L692, N264,
R379.
Cambridge M515.
Cambry B290.
Camelot A102, A103, A113, A114, A266, B21, B178, C429,
G350, H520, M515, P266, S748, T270.
Camlann B773, R206, S11.
See also Battles, Arthur's.
Canamor, King A231.
Canamor y del Infante Turian A231.
Canary Islands P194.
Cancel Leaf B626.
Cancioneros G308.
Canon Law W450.
Cano, Son of Gartnan D159, D160.
'Cantari di Febus-el-Forte' L368.
'Cantari di Liombruno' A90.
'Cantari di Tristano' B313, D105, G243.
Canterbury L670.
'Cantigas de Santa Maria' D49.
Cantre'r Gwaelod B737.
'Canzone d'Amore' G242, S465.
'Capillature' F30.
Caradoc B270, H361, L563, L569, P42, T53.

<16>

Caradoc of Llancarfan   G370, T26.
Caradoc of Vannes   L569.
Carados   H147.
'Carados Brebras'   C349.
Carannog, Saint   K106.
Carantoc   C1.
'Cardenois, Le Roman de'   B344, C250, C251.
Cardueil   D88.
'Carduino'   K364, S902.
Carbonek   S701.
Caritas   R408.
'Carle of Carlisle'   A27, H536, K464, K465.
See also 'Gawain and the Carle of Carlisle'.
Carlisle   C221.
Carmarthen   N28, S832, S833, S834, S836.
See also 'Black Book of Carmarthen'.
'Cassiodorus'   B593.
'Castelain de Couci (Roman du)'   L718.
Castilian Lyric Poetry   D314.
Castleford, Thomas of. See Bek, Thomas.
Castles: General   C350, J158, P232, W346, W347.
 Castellum Puellarum   B421, F266, S445.
 Castle Dore   A267, L32.
 Castle of Corbin   S445.
 Castles of the Grail. See Grail Castles.
 Castleton Garlanding   R309.
 Chateau de Carcelois   C350.
 Chateau de Pesme Aventure   F266, L721, N250, P107, S27.
 Chateau de Pintadol   L721.
 Chateau de Roberon   S27.
 Chateau des Merveilles   C296.
 See also Chateau Merveilleux.
 Chateau des Pucelles   A109, A110, C350, S27.
 Chateau du Roi Pecheur   D90, F419.
 Chateau Merveilleux   L160, Z61.
 Chateau Orgueilleux   M643.
 Chateaux enchantes et leurs Enchantements   P232.
 See also Edinburgh.
 Dinas Emrys 'Hill-Fort'   B680, S103, S104.
 Dolorous Guard   B881, C56, C350, G364, S445.
 Mont-Estreit   F266, L721, S27, S27.
 South Cadbury Castle   A102, A103, A104, A105, A106, A107, A109, A110, A112, A113, A114, A267, T247.
 See also Archaeology.
 Turning Castle   H614.
Castor   C439.
Catalan   B523.
Catalan Literature   G157, O50, P18.
Catalan Poetry   F359, K321.
Catalan Version   P18.
Catalogue Entries   K411.

<17>

Cataloguing S483.
Catalonia B521, P16, R246.
Catguoloph A180, C394, E171, J329, W18.
See also Chat Palu.
'Cath Muighe Tuireadh' O13.
Catharism L131, L157, N74, R479, T123, W235, Z43.
Catharist Heresy O62.
Catigern A239.
Catterick C396.
Caucasian Legends D269.
Cauldron J25, L503.
Cauldron of Plenty B777, B778. P8B,
Cavalcanti, Guido F46, G242, N26, S465.
'Cavalerul Cu Leul' S759.
'Cavalerul Lancelot' S758.
'Cavalleria' R507.
'Cavalleria' and 'Cavallieri' in Chretien M120, M121.
See also Chretien de Troyes.
'Cavallero Zifar' B882, K357, K368, R281, W40.
Cavalon L643.
Cave Legends A1, B6, J250, J283, K378, S827, W293.
See also Lovers' Grotto.
Caw B98.
Caw of Pritdin C118, J285.
Caxton, William   B90A, B390, B391, H303, H578, M148, M240,
M242, M285, M725, N68, N244, S48, S49, S503, S775, V42, V60,
W531, Y3.
'Ceilidhe Iosgaide Leithe' F10, M431.
'Celestina (La)' C90.
Celtic Antiquarianism N253.
Celtic Art D316.
Celtic Britain C129, R183, W458.
Celtic Church C124.
Celtic Civilisation B587, C128, E84, M140.
Celtic Civilisation, Role of Woman in M143.
Celtic Dynastic Themes B745.
Celtic Gods S538, S539.
Celtic Goddesses L527.
Celtic Heathendom R185.
Celtic Heroes S538, S539.
Celtic Hypothesis L550.
Celtic   Influence   D113, F488, H325, M188, O91, R39, R40,
T124, W548, Z3.
Celtic Inscriptions M9.
Celtic Kingdoms D165.
Celtic Language H505.
Celtic Legal Idiom F216.
Celtic Legends B2, B777, E149, E150.
See also Welsh, Irish.
Celtic Literature B115, B749, C115, C122, C128, C132, F13,
G216, H88, H148, J25, M195, N278, R308, S440.
See also Breton, Cornish, Irish and Welsh literature.

<18>

<19>

in Hartmann B512, C314.
in Malory (with reference to Gawain) R514, S572.
of Kahedin in the Prose 'Tristan' B149.
Charlemagne K374, L481, M716, M717.
Charles II of England D176.
Charles VII of France T237.
Charles VIII of France S923.
'Charrette'. See Chretien de Troyes, 'Lancelot'.
Chartres, School of. See School of Chartres.
Chartulary W128.
Chase in Medieval Literature K27, S231, T86.
'Chastelaine de Vergi, La' M122.
Chastiel Bran S445.
Chastity L67, L68, M256.
Chastity Test B152, T130.
Chat Palu F482, G272.
See also Catguoloph.
Chaucer   A236, B166, B886, B933, C154, C260, D116, D216,
F215, F364, G30, G132, H216, H515, H650, J315, K92, K185, K195,
K210, L116, L479, L516, L533, M63, M219, M752, M753, P391, R43,
R367, S117, S183, S185, S582, W323, W324.
 Bibliography G331.
 'Canterbury Tales' M696.
 'Franklin's Tale' A236, D216, F241, L533, P170, R32, S190,
S241.
 'Prioress's Tale' R197.
 'Troilus and Criseyde' G81, S116.
 'Wife of Bath's Tale' A98, B640, C259, C260, E63, E64,
G331, H216, H510, H650, L286, L566, L677, M95, M517, P388,
S495, S793, T239, V31, W359, Z52.
Chauvinism S549.
Chepman and Myllar Prints B169.
Chertsey Tiles H509, L486, L579.
Chester S868.
Chestre, Thomas E174, F474, H158, S208.
 'Sir Launfal'   B431, B435,   D216, E17, H382, H396, K245,
K247, L47, L658, M165, M318, M528, M532, M534, P132, R372,
R445, S47, S190, S457, S880, S881, S908, T259.
'Chevalier a l'Espee'   A47, A244A, J185, J308, N295, O105,
O107, R482.
'Chevalier au Cygne' D221, L427, S2.
'Chevalier au Lion'. See Chretien de Troyes, 'Yvain'.
'Chevalier au Papegau' H360, P48, V38.
'Chevalier aus deus Espees' F204, I39, M714, M755, T82,
V85, W247.
Chevalier Blanc A47.
'Chevalier de la Charette'. See Chretien, and 'Lancelot'.
Chevalier Dore F187.
Chevalier Errant C169, M363, S154.
See also Thomas of Saluzzo.
Chevalier Rouge G297.

<20>

'Chevrefeuille, Chevrefoil, Chevrefueil'. See Marie de France.
Childe Roland A244.
Child in the Tree G316, G317.
Children in Medieval German Literature G300.
China T262.
'Chinon of England' M315.
Chivalric Code of Conduct C314, E46, H130, K99, M124, P167,
W52.
Chivalric Ideals B75, B121, B670, F368, G204, H603, K63,
K291, M177, M235, M251, N98, N99, R59, R260, R511, S393, S643,
W229, W481.
Chivalric Romance B163, C166, G156, H136, H189, K304, L252,
M225, N103, R57, R518, S154, S217, S643, T97.
Chivalry   A119, B90, B113, B146, B152, B153, B154, B156,
B256, B457, B518, B519, B523, B585, B586, B910, C35, C235,
C276, C448, D190, E91, E117, F64, F298, F382, F442, G37, G74,
G212, G342, G368, G402, G403, H184, H197, H198, H216, H306,
H389, H582, J138, K10, K53, K54, K254, K258, K259, K400, K406,
K440, K448, L253, L389, L519, M252, M260, M363, M510, M630,
M633, N45, N46, N48, N49, N51, N52, N53, N98, N99, O82, P19,
P233, P394, R96, R172, R221, R247, R379, R496, R507, S13, S153,
S426, S427, S476, S501, S568, S587, S917, T38, T99, T114, Y10.
 Anti-Chivalric Satire K172.
Chough, Cornish P24.
Chrestomathy T116.
Chrestien or Chretien de Troyes A41, A54, A57, A63, A65,
A71, A129, A183, A194, A233, A281, B14, B33, B34, B130, B164,
B181, B182, B188, B190, B220, B275, B296, B303, B333, B337,
B339, B339A, B344, B345, B447, B461, B581, B654, B664, B729,
B731, B736, B759, B791, B836, B876, C39, C40, C205, C250, C263,
C264, C265, C267, C270, C272, C282, C294, C311, C367, C371,
C400, C403, D99, D114, D266, D307, E87, E92, F4, F117, F201,
F226, F234, F247, F252, F283, F289, F299, F301, F330, F340,
F358, F372, F377, F385, F388, F395, F396, F397, F426, F430,
F434, F435, F454, F462, F524, G21, G32, G53, G75, G117, G118,
G166, G246, G346, G405, G422, G426, G433, G446, G448, G449,
G450, H35, H42, H50, H137, H167, H198, H201, H204, H214, H218,
H221, H223, H232, H272, H279, H297, H298, H418, H421, H424,
H425, H441, H446, H449, H450, H453, H454, H461, H512, H517,
H527, H530, H533, H535, H550, H637, I14, I18, J36, J42, J87,
J148, J155, J254, J255, J295, K40, K42, K43, K72, K81, K88,
K185, K188, K214, K219, K267, K280, K281, K284, K285, K288,
K302, K447, K450, K453, K455, L48, L49, L96, L102, L103, L104,
L105, L160, L169, L221, L222, L223, L228, L230, L243, L292,
L295, L299, L311, L351, L416, L426, L500, L530, L531, L612,
L698, L699, L711, M77, M119, M121, M158, M249, M316, M350,
M356, M411, M432, M434, M439, M440, M441, M472, M475, M477,
M541, M556, M557, M629, M675, M678, N92, N132, N171, N192,
N199, N206, N212, N233, N235, N248, O107, P13, P141, P144,
P157, P184, P188, P336, R73, R83, R87, R88, R96, R99, R128,

<21>

R135, R196, R222, R303, R335, R357, R377, R381, R392, R406,
R420, R421, R426, R454, R536, S31, S32, S62, S117, S152, S208,
S249, S261, S265, S288, S299, S366, S376, S377, S403, S485,
S638, S648, S716, S757, S760, S779, S792, S854, S944, T7, T10,
T45, T62, T69, T114, T183, T206, U6, U8, V4, V14, V48, V95,
V99, V114, W74, W115, W178, W182, W183, W245, W300, W308, W352,
W353, W384, W436, W487, W488, W500, W501, W502, W555, W568,
W575, W651, Z4, Z5, Z6, Z12, Z49, Z71, Z91.
 Bibliography K102, P382.
 'Chansons Courtoises' Z13.
 'Cliges' A130, B32, B192, B284, B296, B303, B304, B954,
C147, C191, C201, C254, D222, F47, F48, F184, F203, F205, F304,
F365, F375, F421, F464, F465, G81, G244, H31, H32, H57, H69,
H70, H238, H425, H446, H453, I36, J42, J69, J71, K3, K88, K290,
L149, L294, L462, L711, M50, M51, M52, M115, M119, M347, M433,
M437, M444, M469, M475, M476, M559, M594, N245, O98, P43, P142,
P158, P164, P248, P314, P348, R88, R119, R133, R361, R363,
R379, S60, S456, S482, T209, U6, V111, W198, W502, Z12.
 'Erec et Enide' A54, A258, B32, B53, B303, B343, B551,
B553, B730, B745, B948, C86, C189, C190, C220, C241, C262,
C324, D97, F202, F205, F236, F261, F263, F364, F410, F413,
F425, F440, G22, G27, G422, G454, G455, G456, H37, H162, H163,
H210, H390, H425, H433, H446, H450, H454, H455, H531, H586,
H587, H598, H599, I21, I42, J42, J227, K18, K19, K27, K39, K87,
K88, K100, K323, K343, K438, L14, L15, L556, L619, L646, L698,
L699, M103, M117, M118, M119, M213, M249, M369, M469, M477,
M479, M495, M541, M543, M630, M643, M671, N129, N217, N219,
N245, N270, N296, P14, P142, P164, P177, P195, P237, P248,
P254, P321, P348, P355, P393, R133, R311, R362, R379, R397,
R424, R436, S60, S61, S63, S476, S519, S664, S713, S942, W341,
W511, W582, W600, W644, Z7, Z8, Z9, Z12, Z32, Z34, Z36.
 'Guillaume d'Angleterre' D15, T258, W505.
 'Lancelot' or 'Knight of the Cart' A42, A57, B81, B128,
B296, B502, B584, B654, B655, B668, C167, C169, C190, C191,
C314, C323, D187, D222, D249, F39, F139, F205, F236, F310,
F311, F421, F429, F430, F436, F438, F455, G22, G54, H34, H399,
H531, H642, I8, I19, I20, I21, I23, J28A, J42, J69, J114, K25,
K88, K95, K96, K97, K325, K326, K327, L12, L16, L38, L54, L98,
L104, L149, L515, L652, L714, L725, M101, M102, M113, M119,
M296, M359, M360, M439, M469, M477, M481, M497, M594, N184,
N259, O21, O106, O108, P22, P38, P158, R11, R20, R21, R22, R88,
R127, R190, R379, R431, R437, R509, R544, R545, R548, R549,
S60, S194, S478, S479, S480, S481, S544, S637, S638, S639,
S640, S713, S890, S894, S906, S917, S945, T10, T48, T209, V9,
V30, V75, V76, V85, V118, W52, W160, W198, W301, Z11, Z12.
 'Perceval' or 'Conte del (du) Graal' A71, A74, A76, A84,
A134, A160, A245, B28, B73, B91, B128, B231, B296, B343, B375,
B398, B654, B711, B712, B787, B794, B870, C6, C59, C60, C61,
C62, C281, C296, C427, C457, D80, D90, D92, D93, D94, E34, E67,
F236, F237, F252, F282, F283, F294, F302, F303, F308, F340,
F369, F370, F376, F381, F384, F387, F394, F399, F402, F415,

<22>

F419, F421, F428, F442, F534, G11, G22, G23, G189, G193, G222,
G224, G225, G241, G259, G260, G315, G341, G359, G364, G422,
G425, G426, G453, G454, G455, H31, H32, H64, H65, H132, H133,
H219, H340, H380, H381, H464, H465, H466, H471, H497, H525,
H636, H639, I14, I16, I22, J69, J154, J159, K4, K7, K41, K82,
K140, K157, K212, K220, K235, K283, K286, K289, K309, K351,
L83, L101, L106, L149, L150, L160, L226, L229, L238, L298,
L300, L303, L304, L384, L444, L483, L510, L546, L567, L580,
L602, L616, L617, L699, L717, L725, M65, M66, M67, M112, M116,
M119, M121, M193, M198, M199, M330, M347, M357, M440, M469,
M470, M477, M699, M700, M701, N125, N139, N206, N208, N229,
N296, O61, O62, O101, O102, O103, O104, O107, P28, P38, P164,
P183, P246, P249, P338, P339, P353, P354, P371, P382, P383, R4,
R14, R127, R169, R192, R193, R194, R248, R264, R290, R291,
R292, R294, R295, R296, R300, R301, R323, R326, R379, R397,
R419, R430, R433, R434, R435, R512, S14, S15, S17, S28, S39,
S40, S60, S286, S301, S308, S367, S407, S544, S709, S714, S781,
S866, S902, S924, T61, T63, T113, T115, T118, T119, T222, U6,
V32, V76, V120, W38, W85, W194, W207, W208, W247, W389, W427,
W489, W491, W492, W493, W495, W603, W639, W640, W656, Z30, Z33,
Z61, Z93.
See also Chretien, Continuators of; and Grail Texts and
Studies.
  'Philomena' B462, D272, H425, H446, Z14.
  'Tristan' B14, B304, H69, H70.
  'Yvain' or 'Knight of the Lion' A39, A56, A130, A257, A258,
A260, B3, B15, B16, B17, B32, B58, B655, B656, B704, B783,
B797, B923, C189, C190, C192, C232, C286, C298, C301, C302,
C309, C323, C324, C345, D190, D222, E140, F136, F139, F184,
F200, F205, F236, F265, F364, F378, F420, F421, G9, G22, G114,
G193, G447, G453, H37, H136, H160, H382, H412, H513, H531,
H599, H638, H641, H646, I23, J42, J69, J135, J182, J183, J227,
J296, J299, K26, K88, K327, K343, K394, L11, L13, L160, L310,
L383, L419, L461, L691, L692, L700, L710, L716, L721, M114,
M119, M213, M216, M296, M328, M360, M469, M477, M593, M750,
N86, N151, N221, N245, N251, N296, P20, P107, P177, P193, P314,
P354, P411, R20, R21, R69, R87, R88, R95, R129, R231, R372,
R379, R387, R432, R438, R440, R510, R558, S53, S60, S68, S188,
S194, S207, S218, S393, S407, S456, S464, S467, S481, S504,
S551, S596, S661, S661A, S665, S667, S717, S730, S759, S785,
S871, S917, T61, T134, U3, U6, W313, W341, W575, W597, W649,
Z10, Z12, Z29, Z31, Z32.
See also Yvain.
Chretien and Germany B191, B192.
Chretien, Continuators of B264, F339, G316, L602, R325,
T113, V95, W491, W492.
See also Gerbert de Montreuil.
  'Perceval Continuations' B270, C253, F393, G12, G14, G17,
L242, L567, L571, M198, M204, M205, M426, P180, P383, R318,
R322, R323, S43, S544, T121, W244, W271.
  'First Continuation' B172, B678, B712, F250, F390, M193,

<23>

P156, S41, V66, W246, W247.
  'Second Continuation' B745, W246, W247.
Chretien's Didactic Aims M479.
Chretien's Humour H31, K222, M357.
Chretien's Imagery G454.
Chretien's Knights M634.
Chretien's Sources R511.
Chretien's Welsh Inheritance G193.
Christ L266, L615.
Christian Background to Secular Narrative L691, W478.
Christian Ideology D36, H582, L287.
Christian Origins V93.
Christian Theology H134, L287.
Christian Virtues and 'Courtaysye' J45.
Christianity C56, F415, H568, L662, M321, N234, S306, T138.
Christianity in Early Britain L347.
'Christus Domini' Concept K218.
'Chronica de Wallia' J261.
'Chronicle of Elis Gruffudd' J277, J279.
'Chronicle of Lanercost' K51, K52.
'Chronicle of the Princes' J288, J289.
Chroniclers, English B657, H578.
Chronicles   A268, B281, C72, C185, E187, F167, F168, G1,
  G115, G179, H493, J186, K50, K51, K52, K344, K372, L634, L635,
  M667, S166, S340, S350, S502, S555, S775, W284, W294, Z39.
'Chroniques Gargantuines'   F342, F343, F344, F345, F346,
  F348, F359.
See also Gargantua and Rabelais.
Chronology B157, B237, B867, F301, F331, F463, H57, H430,
  I11, J46, K327, L301, L302, L700, M119, M576, N95, N111, N179,
  N233, R151, R482, S481, S493, T23, T186, T188, T227, W138,
  W529, W630.
'Chwedlau Cymraeg Canol' J106.
'Chwedlau'r Greal' B750.
'Chwedlau Tegau Eurfon a Thristfardd, Bardd Urien Rheged'
  T94.
'Chwedl Huail ap Caw ac Arthur' J285.
'Chwedl yr Anifeiliaid Hynaf' I2.
'Chwedyl Iarlles y Ffynnawn' T134.
Chwibleian J97.
Cicero N54.
'Cin Dromma Snechta' M16.
Ciry, Michel B206.
Cistercian Influence M291.
Cistercians L157, P149.
'Cite Gaste' L528.
Clairvaux G341.
'Claris et Laris' A131, J314, K182, K229.
Claudas W529.
Clavilles Family F179.
'Cleanness' C99, C211, F209, K333, L156, M683, W508, Z24.

<24>

See also 'Purity'.
'Cleomades' S27.
Clergy B909.
Cliches S795, S947.
Cliges B183, C70, D95, F236, G432, L96, M361, M477, N233, O106, O108, S863.
See also Chretien de Troyes.
'Cliges' (Middle High German) V111.
Closs, Hannah M659.
Clothing M614.
Cocteau, Jean C236, C255, L261.
Coed Celyddon or Coit Celidon C221.
See also Battles.
Coel B161.
Cohen, Gustave M432.
Coins H530, H531.
'Coll Prydain' W15, W36.
Collen, Saint J211.
Colour Symbolism E2, H248, K44, K240, W476.
Coludes Burh C397.
Combat K27.
Combat at the Ford L526, L644.
Comedy. See Humour.
Commentary H107, H113.
Communication (Problems of) P164.
Comparative Literature A127, B38, B589, B590, C155, D264, E45, G381, H62, H267, H362, R147, S372, U8, W1, W216.
'Compert Concula Inn' B319.
'Compert Mongain' M16.
'Complaint of the Black Knight'. See Lydgate.
Composition B946, G27, R192.
'Comte de Poitiers' F7, M90.
'Comus' B423.
'Conculainn' B319.
Condwiramour, Condwiramurs E67, F293, H393.
Congress, Arthurian. See Arthurian Congress.
Congress of Winchester D236, F446, R153.
Connelant N105.
Conquests B101.
Constantine C119.
Constantine, Saint D195, H161.
Constantius Chlorus E43.
'Conte de la Charette'. See Chretien de Troyes and 'Lancelot'.
'Conte del Brait'. See Brait.
'Conte del (du) Graal'. See Chretien de Troyes, 'Perceval' and Grail.
Contes Chevaleresques N250.
'Contes Desrimez' T151.
'Contes Merveilleux' S492.
'Copper Tower' Episode in 'Perlesvaus' W443.
Copyists' Role C168, P264, R300.
'Cor, Lai du'. See 'Lai du Cor'.

<25>

Corbenic B820, M462.
Cornish P24, S570, S571.
Cornish Elements in the Arthurian Tradition P168, S569.
Cornish Legends C176, C177, D150, D196, D201, P168, S733.
Cornish Saints C361, D197, H165.
Cornwall   A215, C361, D180, D181, D194, E72, H165, H317,
H318, H321, H362, J120, J125, J127, J128, J189, L71, N25, Q3,
Q4, S105, T91, W28, W657.
'Coronemenz Loois' L293.
'Corpus Hermeticum' K4, K7.
'Cortaysye' in Middle English E166.
Costa Green, Belle da M540.
Costume B298, C433, E3, G176, L688, T18.
'Couetyse' H389.
Count Philip's Book N199.
See also Chretien de Troyes, 'Perceval'.
'Courrier Arthurien' F380.
'Coup Felon' M208.
Court Poets P70.
Courtesy   B342, B451, B702, C411, E67, F175, G436, K192,
P104, P166, S759, V12.
Courtliness B390, D132.
Courtly Epic B538, D11, H448, J54, L253, M173, R96, R511,
R529.
Courtly Ethic B530, C314, E46, I20, J45, N232, T207.
Courtly Friendship E133.
Courtly Literature   B338, B340, B560, B570, B642, B903,
D283, E44, F291, F359, G392, H266, K84, K177, K280, L442, M258,
M385, M752, N248, R241, R394, R533, R540, S36, S211, S223,
S227, S259, S960, W146, W339, W562, W583.
Courtly Love A172, A201, A276, B4, B131, B156, B247, B334,
B336, B339A, B381, B453, B467, B502, B504, B581, B591, B922,
B946, C142, C237, C260, C279, C314, C341, C343, C348, C411,
C413, C424, D123, D126, D127, D132, D187, D190, D306, F65, F72,
F74, F75, F104, F105, F147, F150, F224, F286, F310, F313, F351,
F397, F407, F423, F427, F429, F430, F435, F439, F532, G4, G41,
G46, G47, G148, G154, G267, G311, G331, G363, G404, G436, H394,
H446, H515, I19, I20, J33, J42, J157, J255, K13, K27, K56, K88,
K99, K185, K192, K210, K305, K330, K358, K394, K458, L51, L82,
L115, L122, L142, L163, L173, L312, L358, L611, M113, M114,
M123, M164, M257, M316, M372, M411, M492, M494, M512, M575,
M587, M604, M626, M629, N40, N42, N76, N128, N288, N289, N290,
N294, O83, P15, P19, P92, P118, P157, P163, P187, P196, P322,
P323, P324, P355, Q7, R66, R121, R156, R177, R189, R257, R447,
R479, R480, R481, R511, R548, S144, S145, S198, S230, S371,
S386, S446, S454, S494, S917, S942, S945, S952, T29, T78, T84,
T235, T243, U4, U6, V110, W98, W198, W199, W242, W281, W343,
W350, W351, W475, W478, W481, W544, W545.
Courtly Motifs M117.
Courtly Romance   B86, B307, B621, C140, C256, C272, D170,
E68, F18, F20, F444, G391, H96, H266, H312, H315, H420, J113,

<26>

K282, K287, L266, M260, M272, M394, M585, R53, R175, R305,
S134, S217, S675, S942, V96, W482, W503, Z51.
Courtly Society A155, B721, E124.
Courtly Vocabulary C294.
Courts of Love K93, L20, L228, M248, N71, R447.
Coward, Handsome A55, B861, B862, B863, B864, M697, W266.
Crashaw, Richard P391.
Crime and Punishment R263.
'Crith Gablach' B357.
Criticism. See Literary Criticism.
Cross, The True A185, C83, F50, G150, S16.
Crowds C205.
Crusade B107, G198, H177, S955.
Cu Chulainn C341, C345, T280.
'Cuento de Tristan' M606, N269.
'Culhwch'. See 'Kulhwch'.
'Culhwch and Olwen'. See 'Kulhwch and Olwen'.
Cunedda H496.
Cunobelin A184, D62.
Cunoworis (Konomor) M100.
Cupid and Psyche A98.
'Curious Discourses' N253.
Curoi T280.
'Cursed Dancers of Colbek' S860.
'Curtana, The' D176, D177.
Curtius, Ernst Robert M82.
Customs K284, K285, L179, T45.
'Cycles of the Kings' D159, R41.
Cymerau, Battle of J80.
Cynfeirdd M136.
'Cynfeirdd a'r Traddodiad Cymraeg, Y' B755.
'Cynon Fab Clydno' R206.
Cywyddau Brud R209.
Czech Literature J59, K242, K243, K244, Z22.
Czech Versions J244, V49.

<27>

Dafydd ap Gwilym   C180, R489.
Dafydd Llwyd   R209.
Dagonet   L87.
'Dame d'Aragon'   P365.
Damen, Mong   W18.
'Damoisele a la Mure'   L296, L297, O82.
Damoiselle Blanche   A47.
'Daniel, Le Livre de'   B643.
Daniel, Samuel   M305.
'Daniel von dem bluehenden Tal'   B648,   G428,   K153,   K271,
L139, L140, M575, R458, W39.
Danish Kings   B234.
Danish History   D14.
Danish Literature   D14, E69, G267.
 Medieval Lyric   F350.
Dante   B25,   B65,   B128,   B355,   C78,   E39,   E177,   G57,   G102,
C170, G309, R258, S530, S531, V12.
 'Convivio'   S531.
 'Divine Comedy   F153, S531.
 'Vita Nuova'   S530.
Darnantes   S821.
'Darogan Myrddin'   P100.
Dathi, Legend of   H493.
Dating   H454, J80, L293, L344, L514, L517, M576, T25, T28,
W407.
 of the Troubadour Rigaut de Barbezieux   L238, V20.
'Dau Gopi O Destun'   E153.
David, Saint   S812, W7, Y11.
'De Audiendis Poetis'   L313.
'De Ave Phoenice'   M16.
'De Consolatione Philosophiae'. See Boethius.
'De Coronatione Arthuri'   H509.
'De Excidio'. See Gildas, Saint.
'De Mirabilius Britanniae'   D135.
'De Nugis Curialium'. See Map, Walter.
'De Officis'   L104, L685.
'De Ortu Walwanii'   B844,   J137,   K397,   M682,   R34,   R35,   T127,
W336.
'De Planctu Naturae'. See Alain of Lille.
'De Re Militari'. See Vegetius.
'De Regimine Principum'   C358.
'De Studio Militari'   L721.
'De Tribus Regibus Mortuis'   T276.
Death, Theme of   K209, L132, L133, R395, U2.
Death of Arthur. See Arthur's Death, 'Morte Arthur',
Malory, and Tennyson.
Decapitation, Theme of   B270, M279.
'Declaration Amoureuse, La'   M361.
'Degare, Sir'   C259, D215, F43, F44, F327, F474, S196, S558,
S881, S882.
'Degrevant, Sir'   C84, F141, H56.

<28>

Deloney, Thomas L114.
'Demanda del Santo Grial' (Spanish) B514, B554, B628, P285, S798.
'Demanda do Santo Graal' (Portuguese) A125, B507, B520, B891, K225, L72, L73, L74, M54, M55, M83, M179, M181, M222, M223, M224, M601, N95, P262, P278, R139, S797.
Demogorgone C338.
Demonic, The F154.
Denis, Saint F360.
Descriptions F132, S157.
Descriptive Technique F107, L710, M66.
'Desire, Lai de'. See 'Lai de Desire'.
Destiny P340.
Devil D137.
'Devil's Barn, The' L126.
Dialectic H646.
Dialects and Forms F473.
Dialogue B156.
'Dialogue of Myrddin and Taliesin' J105.
Diana Nemorensis S759.
Diarmaid L408, L409, L495.
'Diarmaid or Diarmuid and Grainne' C347, K380, N146.
Diarmait Mac Murchadha L336.
Didactisme B466.
'Didot-Perceval' A73, B745, B854, G316, H63, H475, L168, L526, L549, N198, O89, P33, P151, R324, S545, S627, W247.
Dieterich G169.
Dinadan A66, L399, S471, V73, V76.
Dinas Bran L506.
See also Grail Castles.
Dinas Emrys. See Castles.
Dinas Powys A101.
'Dingestow Brut' L321, L383.
'Discourse of Civill Life' L685.
Disguise L688.
Dissertations A218, M733, N140.
'Dittamondo' C354.
'Diu Fossiure in dem Steine' D169.
'Diu Krone'. See Heinrich von dem Tuerlin.
Doble, G. H. R391.
Dodinel le Sauvage
Dodona L311.
Dogma S529.
Dolorous Guard. See Castles.
Dolorous Stroke B775, V66.
Domangart J195.
Dominican Rite H528.
'Don Contraignent' F421.
Don Juan L364.
Don Quixote. See Cervantes.

<29>

'Don Tristan de Leonis'. See Tristan (Spanish).
Donne, John C45.
'Donnei des Amanz' D112, T65.
'Doon, Lay of'. See 'Lay of Doon'.
'Doon de Nanteuil' W127.
'Double Face of Arthur in Layamon' B409.
'Dove's Neck-Ring'. See Ibn Hazm.
'Dover Beach' T260.
'Draco Normannicus' D97, T21.
Dragon C1, F79.
Dramatic Technique L710.
Dramatic Versions F37, L519, N1.
Drayton, Michael C100, G257, G258.
  'Poly-Olbion' M407.
'Dream of Macsen Wledig', 'Dream of Maxen' A5, B708, B756,
M18, O104, O109, T286.
'Dream of Oengus' O104, O109, S463.
'Dream of Rhonabwy' C76, C194, D35, D164, F230, G133, H209,
H353, J199, J204, J205, L667, L668, M18, O75, R201, R203, R206,
R346, R347, T213.
Dream Vision L312, M503.
Dreams B440, E150, G453, S696.
Dreams of Gwenddydd E163.
Drouart La Vache B591.
'Druerie' W124.
Drummer Boy N161.
Dryden, John B626.
  'King Arthur' B626, H231, H400, P391, Y15.
'Duanaire Finn' T94.
Dublin L336.
Duhamel, Georges B206.
'Durmart Le Gallois' B576, B851, C169, G141, G142, K188,
L723, O20, P158, P164, S649, S650, S807, S877, W50, W477.
Dutch 'Ferguut'. See 'Ferguut'.
Dutch 'Lancelot'. See 'Lancelot'.
Dutch Literature B265, C240, D231, D232, D239, D254, D259,
E118, F173, G174, J308, J309, K423, L264, M505, M731, N43,
N273, O100, P5, P12, S683, T79, V36, W277, W551.
See also individual authors and titles.
Dwarfs B167, D87, H190, V30.
Dyfed J223, L336.

<30>

'Early Brittany' C130.
Early Languages J17.
Earthly Paradise L86.
East German Romance T88.
Ebraucus H663.
Ecclesia-Synagoga Theme F415, H65.
'Echtra Condla' 093.
Echtrae and Immram D292.
'Ecidemon' S487.
'Ecke, Chanson D'' Z70.
Ecu K43.
'Edda' J233, K159, W6.
'Edeles Herze' K458, S694.
Edinburgh B421.
See also Castles: Castellum Puellorum.
Edition of Texts K208, L703, R123.
Editions (Old) K320, P260, V42, W586, W590.
Edmond, Saint M302.
'Edolan' S237.
Education C357.
Education of Girls, The C308.
Education of the Hero in Arthurian Romance C358.
Edward I L402A, L538, L541, M610.
Edward III D188, K62.
Edward IV K125.
'Eger and Grime' C13, D318, S190.
'Egilssaga' S68.
'Eglamure' H56.
Egyptian Influence H153, H154, H156.
Eilhart von Oberg B276A, B659, B942, C336, D117, E24, E25,
E40, F462, G232, G438, H458, K417, L169, L468, M735, P300,
R121, S195, S435, S687, S883, S884, W41, W632.
  'Eneide' P236.
  'Tristrant' B49, B198, B200, B276A, B659, B942, B943, B944,
B946, B947, B949, B954, B955, D65A, D66, D87, E141, F58, F59,
F71, F280, F406, F407, G128, H466, H479, H615, K242, L148,
L216, L230, L352, P230, P236, P316, R372, R503, R511, S159,
S195, S257, T67, W42, W305, W549, W550.
Eleanor of Aquitaine C142, K93, K94, L3, L228, L230, R447,
V95, W64, W438.
Elfin Chronicle B887, D313, K115, Y2.
Eliot, T. S. D4, K268, M619, M625, V43.
  'Prufrock' R522.
  'The Waste Land' B288, C415, D1, D4, F225, G95, K139, K329,
M623, N85, P9, P391, R78, S573, V44, W141, W448, W449.
Elis Gruffydd F217.
'Elis Saga' H52, H54.
Eliseg, Pillar of M8.
Elizabethan Drama M106.
Elizabethan Fiction P117.
Elizabethan Themes A248.

'Elucidation, The'   P339, P383, T118, T119.
Eluned   T95.
Emain Ablach   C188.
'Emare, Lay of'.   See 'Lay of Emare'.
Embroideries   S342, S343.
Emerson, R. W.   A52, C25, R97, W326.
Empedocles   G278.
Emrys Wledig   J85.
Emyr   L411.
Enanchet   F104, F224, M728, P410, V92.
Enchanted Forests.   See Forests.
Enchantress   063.
'Eneas'   B954,   C348,   F463,   F507,   G271,   G303,   H424,   H427,
H436, H458, I11, L98, L269, M437, O72.
'Eneit'.   See Heinrich van Veldeken.
'Enfances' (Theme)   M330, W643.
'Enfances Gauvain'   K397, L533, M427, T127.
'Enfances Guiron'   B492.
'Enfances Lancelot'   B179, B610, B612, B614, B615, B880.
Engels, Robert   B203.
English Alliterative Poems   H268, L448, S258.
English Alliterative Romances   L566, O58.
English Arthuriana   A19.
English Ballads   G276.
English Chroniclers   H578.
English Court   L105.
English Folklore   066.
English Literature   A152, A243, B43, B45, B115, B719, B963,
D149, D295, G161, H250, K372, L117, L197, M29, M674, P172,
P223, P391, R140, R148, S457, S730, S776, T46, T277, W351,
W361.
 Early   B774, H56, M44.
 Medieval A13, A14, A21, A115, A243, B135, B136, B137, B138,
B166, B356, B429, B534, B573, B618, B877, B878, B924, C259, D7,
D170, D171, D272, D273, D299, E3, E70, E173, E174, E175, F215,
F233, F473, G161, G212, H12, H152, H283, H401, H633, K28, K337,
L67, L68, L86, L116, L195, L249, L389, L456, L512, M693, N266,
O112, O116, O117, P218, P317, R230, R445, S141, S185, S190,
S385, S457, S549, S699, S860, S878, T112, T198, T199, T200,
T201, T202, T203, T259, U18, V115, W142, W222, Z96.
See also individual authors and works.
 Modern   E35, E36, H58, M618, S723, W620.
English Legal Customs   Y11.
English Poets   M35, M273.
English Politics   M62.
English Renaissance Epics   B45.
English Sources   R265.
English Tradition   N145.
English Victorian Poetry   G278.
See also individual authors and works.
Enide   B743, C86, H210, H586, L100, S63.
Enigma   M330, Z94.
Ensenhamen   O83.

<32>

'Enserrement Merlin' B837.
See also Merlin.
Entrelacement D107, D108.
Enygeus I15, N224.
Eochaid Aingces P1.
Eon de L'Etoile F265, L134.
Epic   A61, B158, C18, D204, G436, I41, K316, L381, M587,
P334, P354, S426, S427, S643, U12, V72, V104, Z6.
Epic Cycles T112.
Epic Formulae A269.
'Epic Quest' C18.
Epic Time-scale in Chretien and Wolfram W200, W201.
Epic structure in Hartmann von Aue L381.
Equality in Love K27.
Equitan D87.
See also Marie de France.
Equivocal Oaths H365.
Erec B734, G428, G441, K237, L317, L666, M478, M500, M742,
O21, R141, W346, W436.
'Erec', Prose B511, P269.
See also Chretien de Troyes and Hartmann von Aue.
'Erec and Enide'   B226, F139, F421, G193, J150, L99, M555,
M742, P131.
'Erec et Enide'. See also Chretien de Troyes.
'Erexsaga' B387, B388, G441, K17, K18, K19, Z32.
Erfurt Historiated Cloth V21.
See also Iconography.
'Erikskroenika' B411, J73.
'Erkenwald, Saint' P395.
Ermatiger G328.
Ermonie B850.
Eros B34.
Erotic Language M535.
Erskine, John T249.
'Eructavit' M495.
'Esboniad Cymraeg Ar Broffwydoliaeth Myrddin' R330.
See also Merlin.
'Eschacier' F534.
Esclarmonde K182, W127.
'Escoufle (L')' L718, P315, R482, V21.
See also Jean Renart.
'Esmoreit' P211.
Esotericism G411.
'Espinette Amoureuse'. See Froissart.
'Esplandian' M84.
Esplumoir Merlin A73, B793, L459, N198.
See also Merlin.
'Esprover', Meaning of Z9.
Essays in Honour of. See Festschriften.
'Estoire del Saint Graal'. See Grail.
'Estoire dou Graal'. See Robert de Boron.

<33>

Estregales B843.
Estrildis T24.
Esyllt. See Iseult.
Etain B286, B434.
Ethelred's Laws Y11.
Ethelred The Unready A104.
'Ethica' H645.
Ethics K54, S767, S768.
Ethiopian Legend S778.
Etrekeltiek, Sant M525.
Etymology D97, H393, K315, N201, S727.
Eucharist B520, B772, C4, F211, L612, R245, R314.
Eufemia Ballads B411, F349, S107.
'Eufemiavisor' H648, S107.
European Literature A284, B71, C451, C452, F68, K21, K415, R147, V34.
Evans, Sebastian D301.
Evil S333.
Evrain M369.
Ewert, Alfred S908.
Excalibur A215, B771, C50, D176, E149, H209, H366, J124, L344, L345, L398, L643, S814, V67.
'Excidio et Conquestu Brittaniae, De'. See Gildas.
Example R141.
Exemplum S191.
Exile of the Sons of Uisliu G359, H632.
Extasy T261

<34>

<35>

Adolf, Helen A235, B149, B666, C350, G6, N149, P157, P320, R506, S654, T40, W546, W581.

Ammann F79A.

Attisani, Adelchi G429.

Beissner, Friedrich S204.

Beyschlag, Siegfried F82, G41.

Boor, Helmut De F83, F84, G42, K458, M591, N114, O8, P398.

Boutiere, Jean B150, F427.

Bruneau, Charles M332.

Brunel, Clovis M333.

Clapton, G. T. B384, E143.

Crozet, Rene F293, F419, G15, M209, R87, R495.

Delbouille, Maurice C20, M334.

Eggers, Hans B567, E113.

Ewert, Alfred S908.

Finsterwalder, Karl R454.

Foerste, William C78, R498.

Ford, J. D. M. S909.

Fourquet, Jean F419, H601, M264, M335, V75, W86, Z70.

Frappier, Jean D189, L92, M121, M337.

Gamillscheg, Ernst K431, L643.

Gardette, Pierre D89, M338.

Giese, Wilhelm W50.

Halbach, Kurt Herbert F466, P215, S129.

Hamburger, Kaete F85, S391.

Harmer, Charles C300.

Hoepffner, Ernest M340.

Horacek, Blanka H214.

Imbs, Paul D98, F434, L149.

Karg-Gasterstaedt, Elisabeth

Kastner, Leon E. R469, S910.

Kluckhohn, Paul F86.

Kohlschmidt, Werner F98, M262, W186, W187.

Kralik, Dietrich F87.

Kunstmann, John G. F88, F89.

Kunz, Josef S322.

Labande, Edmond-Rene M341.

Lecoy, Felix B151, C167, D99, G123, G359, I23, K36, M473, N252.

Le Gentil, Pierre D97, F268, F432, G24, G358, J302, L93, L428, M342, M472, M599, P158, P266, P315, R191, S63, S864, S924.

Lejeune, Rita M343, M471.

Lewis, C.S. B702.

Linder, Kurt E58.

Loomis, Gertrude Schoepperle L574.

Loomis, Roger Sherman S911.

MacNeill, Eoin S912.

Markman, Alan S62.

Maurer, Friedrich F80.

Meritt, Herbert Dean A25, B124, F93, H264, J100, K173.

Michaelsson, Karl M344.

<36>

Mohr, Wolfgang D205, F90.
Monteverdi, Angelo S907.
Moser, Hugo K152.
Mosse, Fernand M345.
Muehler, Robert F91, H556.
Nagel, Bert A83.
Nitze, William Albert S913.
Norman, Frederick S914.
Oehmann, Emil F92.
Panzer, Friedrich N113.
Parry, John Jay S915.
Pellegrini, Silvio F47, R88.
Pope, Mildred K. S916.
Pretzel, Ulrich F81.
Reichardt, Konstantin B325, F93.
Roques, Mario M346.
Rostaing, Charles A285, C96, F436, J304, L83, S925.
Rubio i Balaguer, Jordi E145.
Santangelo, Salvatore V100.
Sato, Teruo M347.
Schlauch, Margaret J283.
Schroebler, Ingeborg B568, F94, F509, S288, S320, S390.
Schroeder, Werner P329.
Seidler, Herbert W628.
Siciliano, Italo B58, B409, C403, L572, M469, S53.
Spitzer, Leo H195.
Thomas, J. Heywood G193.
Thompson, A. W F95.
Trier, Jost F96.
Tschirch, Fritz W598.
Utley, Francis Lee B138, J42, K35, M240.
Vinaver, Eugene M551.
Wagner, Kurt F81A.
Walberg, Emmanuel M348.
Weber, Gottfried B633, F97.
Weevers, Theodor W220.
Wehrli, Max B918, F98, H9, M263, R513.
Whitehead, Frederick B402, B506, D190, K137, M480, R474,
S479, S917, T51, T152, V79.
Willoughby, Leonard Ashley R226, S918.
Zinsli, Paul F99.
Feudal Background A77.
Feudal Oath D205.
Feudal Society M685.
Feudality C170, H5.
Feval, Paul D184.
Fier Baiser L539, R494.
'Fierabras' H266, H568.
Fin'Amor. See Courtly Love.
Finistere W102.
Finn L670, S410.

<37>

Fir Bolg L345.
Fisher King   A82, B865, B870, C52, D90, F415, F419, K387,
K392, M469, N173, N194, N204, N209, O61, R476, W141.
See also Roi-Pecheur.
Fitz-Osborn, William L347.
Fitzgerald, F. Scott, 'The Great Gatsby' G416.
'Five Dreams of Ganiedd' W63.
'Flamenca' B836, G347, K322, L109, L240, L241, L306, M512,
R160, W199, W370.
Flanders L671.
'Fled Bricrend' T280.
'Flegetanis' H393, R245, R248.
Flemish Literature F521.
Flemish 'Percheval' F521, M503.
Flintshire County Library H148, H149.
'Floire et Blancheflor' D77, H35, R482.
See also Blancheflor-Perceval Question, and Blanscheflur.
Florence Romance Heroine S722.
'Flores Historiarum' H509.
'Floriant et Florete', 'Floriant et Florette' L55, W380,
W381, W391.
'Florimont, Le Roman De' B643.
'Floris and Blancheflour' S860.
Folie. See Madness.
'Folie Lancelot' M364, W603.
'Folie Tristan' A59, B212, B343, B511, E141, F354, H415,
H417, H565, H566, J147, J298, L245, M656, R364, T64, V4.
'Folie Tristan' (Berne) D55, D112, F57, F408, H415,
H416, H444, H565, H566, J147, K36, K183A, L181, L693, M364,
M656, P165, R355, R364, S935, T64.
'Folie Tristan' (Oxford) D112, H36, H416, H445, J147,
L181, L693, M364, P165, P314, R364, S353, S935, W660, Y13.
Folk Heroes H506.
See also Hero.
Folklore   A98, A99, A215, B285, B455, B539, B621, B708,
B813, B962, C176, C194, C258, C355, C358, C434, D16, D17, D73,
D79, D177, D184, D211, D269, E100, E117, F8, F88, F89, F169,
F327, G206, G317, G351, G399, H249, H350, H448, H477, J25,
J145, J217, J224, J242, J250, J258, J281, K106, K325, K361,
K369, L6, L94, L95, L126, L552, M21, M22, M165, M231, M405,
N205, N278, N279, N281, P93, P109, R16, R17, R18, R105, R186,
R208, R275, R445, R466, S203, S420, S700, S702, S733, S778,
S818, S826, S959, T19, T45, T90, T91, T129, T130, T191, T208,
U14, U15, U16, V43, W434, W537.
 Index of Folklore T129, T130.
See also Celtic material.
Food Imagery in 'Queste Del Saint Graal' B533.
Fool M364, N264.
'Forain' L147.
Forests G453, W422.
 Enchanted F257.

<38>

See also Broceliande, Caledonian Forest, and Morrois, Forest of.
Form   E92, G263, M128, R531, R546, W476.
Formula   C257, H511, J166, W59.
Fornication   M478.
Fortuna   B569, H413, P137.
Fortunate Isles   B259.
Fortune   E6, P254.
Foscolo   B61.
'Fouke Fitz Warin'   S445.
See also Fulk Fitzwarin.
Foulet, Lucien   F51.
Fountain Episode   J183, M665.
Fountain of Life   C331.
'Four Ancient Books of Wales'   S546.
Fournier, Alain, 'Le Grand Meaulnes'   B129.
Fox-Hunts   M419, T85.
Fragonard   M608.
Franc-Palais   F187, F189.
Francesca   H194.
Francisco de Morais   L77, M174.
Franco-Dutch Relations   G107.
Franco-English Culture   B335.
Francois I   S923.
Frank, Istvan   B117, M336.
Franks Casket, The   A239.
Frappier, Jean   J160, M362.
'Frauendienst'   H234, P118, R130, T102.
See also Courtly Love.
Frazer, James G., 'The Golden Bough'   V43.
Frederick of Normandy   T172.
Freidank   R67.
Fremstad, Olive   C454.
French Anthology   W43.
French Arthurian Scholarship   W383.
'French Book'. See Malory.
French Civilisation in 'Mabigonion'   W132.
French Language   H332, I18, M332, R253, S939.
French Legends   M220.
French Literature   B70, B592, B676, C82, C88, C255, C266,
C273, C400, D68, E14, G89, G216, G361, H159, H218, H331, H438,
H534, J108, M482, M542, M751, N255, O59, P140, P199, P257,
P301, S338, V123, W58, W586, Z91.
 Medieval   B213, B429, B439, B627, C271, C272, C280, C402,
C414, D288, F78, F117, F185, F250, F304, F356, F400, G31, H530,
H531, J155, K282, K287, K455, L180, L301, L302, M488, M506,
M519, M548, M607, M684, M752, N158, P146, P159, R158, R251,
R263, R394, R465, S385, T116, T186, T188, V9, W245, W587, W588,
W589, W591, W643.
 Old   A61, F17, U4, U5, U6, V123.

<39>

Gab R134.
'Gabail in t'Sida' H631.
Gaheret V57.
Gahmuret B906, G303, H393, M397, S4, S781, S954.
Gaimar, Geffrei B229, B232, B233, B234, K372, T33.
 'Estoire des Engleis' B230, B237, B240, K75, M368, W75.
 'Haveloc' B239.
Galaad. See Galahad.
Gaheriet B405.
Galabes W18.
'Galagrus and Gawane' H344.
Galahad   A168, A179, A244, B800, B819, C162, D208, D298,
E75, K103, K104, L496, L620, M347, M666, R514, S625, W57, W272,
W529.
'Galehaut' B612, C70, F409, F440, Z60.
Galeotto G58.
'Galeran de Bretagne' D278, F244, F245, F246, F247, F251,
H423, L64, L718, L719, P200, P315, W488.
See also Jean Renart.
Galerous H566.
Galeschin L721.
Galice B621, R245.
Galiot S146.
Gallican Liturgy Q2.
Galloway D93, D98, W163.
Galoain H586.
Galvoie C60.
Gamarien, Guimarant L148.
Ganelon T228.
'Gangandi Greidi' F213.
Ganieda P122.
Ganiedd W63.
Ganole J165.
'Garel'. See Pleier, Der.
Gareth A162, G417, W529.
'Gareth' G297.
'Gareth, Sir' O104.
'Gareth, The Tale of' A22, A25, D45, S215.
Gareth of Orkeney, Sir D173, S207.
'Gareth and Lynette' S460.
Gargantua B798, F347, G326.
See also 'Chroniques Gargantuines'.
'Garin de Monglane' S877.
'Garin Le Loherin' J69, P336.
Garter, Order of the R172.
Gaul D165.
'Gauriel von Muntabel' G428, K271, L140.
Gautier d'Arras   C368,   C369,   C371, D99, H272, P88, R75,
S859.
 'Eracle' G457, R88, R90, R175.
 'Ille et Galeron' C286, C364, C365, C370, C372, C373, G457,

<41>

H437, M250, N296, R75, R88, R177, R177.
Gautier Espec L187.
Gautier Map. See Map, Walter.
Gawain A20, A23, A24, A26, A67, A162, B74, B84, B90, B266A,
B270, B280, B364, B375, B403, B404, B405, B475, B477, B530,
B625, B699, B701, B745, B833, B906, B935, C59, C60, C74, C99,
C143, C208, C210, C296, C332, D8, D26, D53, D72, D229, D249,
E1, E6, E86, E104, E118, E167, E169, F35, F119, F120, F261,
F263, F296, F390, F393, G12, G17, G192, G207, G260, G306, G310,
H297, H335, H356, H366, H370, H389, H582, H643, H644, I4, I29,
J4, J45, J145, J176, J178, J185, J216, K1, K49, K55, K99, K192,
K193, K219, K278, K313, K389, L89, L90, L197, L260, L287, L385,
L460, L496, L498, L516, L520, L533, L566, L570, L680, M48, M59,
M63, M79, M151, M169, M193, M198, M209, M210, M261, M279, M288,
M317, M330, M415, M526, M527, M530, M584, M614, M642, M682,
M723, M742, N212, O103, O104, O105, P173, P228, P281, P325,
P331, P362, R15, R76, R121, R290, R292, R323, R328, R473, S4,
S33, S41, S117, S155, S409, S466, S476, S497, S587, S622, S628,
S685, S689, S854, T35, T77, T126, T127, T223, W16, W52, W70,
W253, W257, W290, W291, W292, W323, W324, W679, Z98.
Gawain and Aeneas D27.
Gawain and Michaelmas P8.
'Gawain and the Carle of Carlisle' A22, A27, H536, K464,
K465, M48, R445, S47, T53, W507.
'Gawain and the Green Knight' A2, A18, A20, A24, A96, A158,
A159, A237, B54, B72, B83, B85, B93, B139, B160, B162, B165,
B268, B269, B294, B295, B403, B404, B445, B556, B582, B583,
B636, B701, B702, B707, B726, B730, B877, B883, B929, B930,
B932, B935, B936, B937, B938, B939, B958, C44, C73, C75, C102,
C143, C149, C150, C152, C153, C178, C198, C207, C208, C209,
C211, C212, C213, C214, C215, C284, C312, C317, C322, C329,
C375, C387, C439, D27, D37, D48, D72, D144, D213, D230, D297,
D304, E1, E2, E70, E71, E88, E89, E166, E169, E170, E175, F2,
F108, F151, F195, F210, F222, F314, F363, F491, F493, G28, G35,
G61, G64, G65, G100, G101, G102, G208, G213, G214, G263, G277,
G310, G320, G322, G374, G375, G430, H12, H40, H41, H49, H59,
H60, H61, H68, H142, H166, H239, H240, H249, H294, H309, H344,
H364, H368, H369, H370, H371, H384, H386, H538, H581, H582,
H583, H621, H627, J1, J3, J45, J60, J131, J145, J175, J216,
J237, J256, K1, K35, K90, K138, K147, K178, K179, K192, K193,
K194, K296, K333, K335, K336, K381, K386, L1, L34, L72, L73,
L74, L130, L156, L284, L287, L327, L431, L460, L484, L524,
L580, L582, L657, L696, M26, M27, M48, M58, M60, M110, M150,
M154, M232, M233, M235, M236, M278, M288, M302, M318, M383,
M384, M414, M419, M526, M614, M615, M621, M634, M637, M691,
M692, N4, N59, N160, N163, N271, O1, O2, O4, O5, O67, O68, O69,
O74, P7, P8, P169, P171, P205, P216, P223, P281, P319, P352,
P361, P363, P395, R12, R44, R45, R116, R140, R168, R169, R170,
R197, R210, R229, R262, R267, R309, R445, R446, R486, S23, S37,
S38, S57, S79, S80, S81, S82, S83, S84, S85, S86, S87, S88,
S89, S90, S91, S92, S93, S95, S96, S97, S98, S137, S142, S197,

<42>

<43>

<44>

H477, I34, I35, J32, J196, J229, J310, J329, K30, K78, K79, K80, K165, K166, K174, K254, K258, K259, K260, K261, K304, K405, L108, L348, L350, L443, L453, M547, M548, M566, M582, M684, M687, N45, N46, N48, N49, N52, N53, O99, P236, R220, R227, R533, S19, S46, S59, S200, S211, S224, S266, S281, S388, S525, S659, S873, V119, W84, W183, W232, W629.
See also Gottfried von Strassburg, Hartmann von Aue, Wolfram von Eschenbach.
 Modern D153, H268, M582, S161.
 Old K320.
German Princes B568.
German Tradition S590.
Germany B188, K251.
Gernemudhe S578, S581.
Gerontius J86, L666.
Gervase of Tilbury C376, O66.
'Gesta Danorum' S552, T214.
'Gesta Hammaburgensis Ecclesiae Pontificum' M718.
'Gesta Pilati' M203.
'Gesta Regum Anglorum'. See William of Malmesbury.
'Gesta Romanorum' L155.
'Geste de Boun de Hamton' W133.
'Geste des Loherains' B627.
'Geste des Normanz'. See Wace.
Giants A94, D87, F133, F153, J25, L46.
'Giglan (L'Hystoire de)' A47.
Gildas, Saint A147, A148, A225, B558, B689, B723, B925, C95, C112, D152, E122, F26, F472, H624, J193, J194, J269, K140, L339, L601, L632, M670, N159, R103, R202, S850, S851, T93, T176, W12, W22, W23, W31, W36, W283.
 'De Excidio et Conquestu Britanniae' E157, G371, L566, L601, O95, W19.
 'Vita Gildae' B791, C137, F26, G268, L244, W664.
'Gilgamesh' K246, W221.
Gilion S781.
Gilson, Etienne M339.
'Gingembras' L722.
Ginover G376.
Giraldus Cambrensis C45, G182, J266, S7, T8.
'Girart of Roussillon' H13, M744.
Girault, Francois B798.
'Girone il Cortese' T14.
Glamorgan A101.
Glastonbury A261, A262, A264, A267, B289, B543, B544, B545, B546, B547, B811, C55, C137, C162, C352, D175, D201, F23, F25, F26, G298, G403, H98, H351, H363, H559, I33, L30, L328, L329, L396, L566, L594, M183, M185, M206, M470, N126, N172, N177, N188, R7, R8, R368, R369, R371, S559, S560, S828, S834, S879, T246, T247, T269, V91, W7, W27, W128, W134, W442.
'Glastonbury Legends, The' L24, L26, T247.
'Gliglois' L401, L718.
Glossary S855.
Glosses H333, M498.

<45>

Gloucester K184.
God A276, R58.
Goddess, The White G274.
Godefroi de Leigni A42.
Godefroid de Bouillon D221.
Godefroy de Viterbo, 'Pantheon' M424.
Godmund T53.
'Gododdin'. See Aneirin, Aneurin.
Gods S538, S539.
Goethe B24, B25, G92, H45, H277.
 'Faust' R235.
Gog B812.
Gog and Magog S957.
Gogulor F180.
Goidels O77.
'Golagros and Gawain'   B84, B169, B796, C380, H539, K157,
L86, R229, S808, T277.
Good Priest S9.
Goodness B365.
'Gorboduc' W139.
Goreu M41.
Gormond C181, S646.
Gormont B950.
'Gormont et Isembart' A254.
Gornemant C60, G260, J158.
Gorre, Kingdom of B840, F310, K96, M469, O106.
'Gospel of Philip the Deacon' B545.
'Gospel of the Infancy' W385.
'Gotfrid Hagens Reimchronik' P236.
Gottfried von Strassburg A9, A140, A249, B18, B26, B126,
B175, B325, B360, B361, B362, B465, B559, B563, B567, B609,
C234, D117, D140, D154, E32, E40, E105, F127, F194, F462, F466,
F485, F504, F505, G40, G83, G232, H46, H192, H214, H269, H271,
H311, J30, J35, J36, J40, J68, J75, J109, J196, J228, J310,
K80, K186, K204, K205, K255, K260, K276, K324, K332, K408,
K443, K458, L40, L41, L169, L442, M255, M257, M320, M379, M406,
M686, M694, M707, N43, N119, N162, N261, O10, O12, P189, P252,
P300, R49, R55, R384, R441, S106, S135, S170, S172, S219, S245,
S246, S250, S251, S275, S303, S304, S381, S398, S435, S528,
S675, S687, S753, T62, W2, W65, W151, W155, W179, W183, W335,
W536, W569, W595, W601, W655, W666, Z25, Z46, Z79.
 Bibliography S804.
 'Tristan' A144, A230, A276, B49, B123, B127, B175, B180,
B198, B223, B326, B363, B402, B450, B451, B466, B564, B565,
B566, B589, B866, B890, B959, C46, C107, C193, C206, C225,
C233, C288, C303, C305, C425, C426, D10, D87, D146, D147, D155,
D156, D157, D166, D169, E32, E45, E52, E54, E95, E113, E123,
E141, F55, F59, F71, F83, F287, F288, F292, F466, F485, F508,
F509, F516, F531, G40, G42, G113, G148, G166, G169, G171, G177,
G183, G185, G264, G266, G380, G387, G389, G390, G391, G392,
G393, G412, H26, H27, H28, H43, H123, H165, H184, H187, H208,

<46>

H222, H226, H228, H229, H233, H285, H311, H346, H348, H354,
H355, H368, H476, H479, H514, H596, H600, H652, I32, J37, J38,
J39, J41, J50, J51, J53, J168, J328, J331, K33, K53, K158,
K201, K202, K223, K281, K295, K310, K311, K314, K318, K342,
K461, L53, L289, L316, L317, L580, M152, M157, M229, M265,
M324, M406, M425, M507, M574, M582, M588, M595, M651, M657,
M689, N7, N38, N110, N111, O8, O45, O72, P176, P192, P206,
P209, P227, P250, P316, Q7, Q8, R52, R59, R60, R62, R63, R121,
R236, R395, R444, R449, R495, R499, R503, R511, R527, S6, S109,
S127, S139, S159, S212, S220, S239, S247, S248, S257, S294,
S307, S313, S322, S325, S370, S381, S383, S389, S390, S402,
S404, S437, S489, S594, S595, S694, S695, S718, S719, S746,
S779, S789, S790, S799, S800, S805, S872, S884, T36, T56, T83,
T250, T263, T264, T265, V7, V8, W1, W46, W87, W96, W97, W98,
W99, W150, W152, W154, W186, W227, W457, W473, W474, W475,
W481, W570, W572, W599, W666, W673, Y11, Z2, Z26, Z74, Z76.
'Gottweiger Trojanerkrieg' L140.
Gower F151.
'Gowther, Sir' M534, O25.
Gozzi S36.
'Graelent'. See 'Lai de Graelent'.
'Graelentmor' M673.
Grail A24, A78, A80, A130, A141, A143, A151, A169, A170,
A172, A173, A177, A185, A190, A191, A213, B29, B31, B45A, B45A,
B60, B65, B67, B92, B107, B130, B222, B289, B310, B314, B345,
B372, B375, B398, B437, B441, B442, B448, B484, B491, B506,
B508, B509, B514, B522, B544, B545, B576, B577, B588, B639,
B668, B681, B682, B684, B685, B687, B778, B785, B788, B790,
B852, B875, B891, B906, B912, B915, B916, B949, C4, C27, C59,
C60, C78, C93, C138, C139, C163, C202, C238, C258, C297, C310,
C330, C331, C353, C377, C434, D1, D54, D63, D74, D75, D94,
D142, D193, D200, D265, D296, D298, D306, D317, E15, E16, E90,
E92, E108, E164, E176, E177, E178, E179, E180, E181, F13, F14,
F32, F142, F192, F211, F252, F283, F297, F299, F322, F369,
F370, F371, F376, F379, F382, F387, F419, F424, F428, F431,
F442, F528, G29, G55, G67, G72, G77, G119, G153, G201, G203,
G223, G224, G225, G234, G237, G246, G261, G279, G288, G289,
G325, G362, G409, G410, G411, G414, H23, H74, H97, H140, H202,
H254, H277, H281, H290, H316, H345, H377, H379, H439, H528,
H535, H545, H558, H669, H670, H671, I14, I31, I33, J36, J57,
J145, J162, J170, J177, J203, J241, J243, J248, J317, J319,
J322, J323, K2, K7, K9, K108, K120, K215, K272, K278, K332,
K411, K418, K435, K457, L19, L25, L27, L29, L30, L117, L221,
L222, L256, L263, L279, L311, L369, L428, L496, L501, L503,
L506, L509, L510, L532, L543, L544, L578, L602, L612, L613,
L614, L615, L648, L661, M33, M34, M36, M69, M177, M182, M183,
M184, M187, M222, M230, M261, M291, M392, M393, M395, M396,
M405, M429, M440, M441, M445, M446, M450, M453, M470, M486,
M562, M602, M620, M622, M649, M720, M743, M758, N2, N75, N78,
N94, N95, N125, N172, N176, N185, N199, N201, N206, N209, N210,
N215, N227, N230, N280, N281, N283, N284, N287, O28, O32, O50,

<47>

O62, O89, O103, O104, P8B, P20, P46, P52, P135, P136, P143, P144, P145, P147, P160, P284, P285, P286, P320, P326, P327, P329, P366, P367, P373, R15, R24, R25, R26, R51, R59, R121, R192, R216, R258, R259, R265, R266, R307, R323, R393, R396, R398, R417, R425, R426, R429, R439, R512, R516, S4, S16, S40, S41, S43, S77, S178, S203, S209, S289, S292, S346, S419, S422, S438, S461, S527, S537, S563, S662, S701, S727, S750, S772, S774, S791, S840, S855, S867, S956, T73, T115, T118, T119, T246, T250, T252, V27, V47, V65, V85, V91, V93, V94, V120, W53, W54, W55, W56, W57, W157, W197, W207, W208, W246, W247, W260, W261, W267, W273, W312, W318, W344, W364, W385, W429, W442, W489, W491, W492, W493, W497, W498, W501, W603, W608, W621, W626, Z20, Z59, Z63, Z98.

'Graal, Le Contes Del' A82, B398, C60, F415, H133, J158, M119, M357, M643, N175, P38.

'Graal, Estoire Del Saint' B82, B838, C162, H503, K245, L27, M467, O28, P52, S630, S864, V46.

'Graal, Roman du' (Post-Vulgate) B478, P160, V41, W173, W304.

'Petit Saint Graal' H607

Grail Castles A97, C56, D302, F442, G15, G341, G364, H277, L506, M192, M277, M469, N174, N222, O61, O62, O102, P212, R323, S14, S445, S709, S736, S770, W88, W195, W257, W603, Z17.

Grail Colloquy L225, N78, R400, R422.

Grail Cycle B517, M207, V46.

Grail King B491, G376, M469, S25, W462.

Grail Knight G228, R514.

Grail Legend A81, B398, B750, B792, D36, D90, F153, F225, F442, J324, L238, L304, L366, L547, L562, L565, L571, L717, M207, M270, M329, N133, O62, O104, P182, R243, R245, R298, R299, R323, R505, S4, S362, S508, S529, S715, S747, S849, T117, T286, V5, V26, W53, W169, W170, W172, W237, W238, W307, W310, W571, W603, Z16.

(Italian Version) B314.

(Spanish Version) P283, P286.

Grail Manuscript O28.

Grail Messenger K393.

Grail Motifs G416, R522.

Grail Mountain G72, L248, P212.

Grail Origin H316, M194, S421.

Grail Poetry C432, K280, M138, N225.

Grail Problem W440.

Grail Procession F360.

Grail Quest G421, K225, K246, L595, M198, R308, S62, S501, V98, W188, W261.

In modern art and literature B912.

See also 'Queste del Saint Graal'.

Grail Romances A76, B384, B400, B491, D92, F462, H207, H286, H446, J20, K224, L23, M210, N173, N178, N179, N203, N282, O89, P246, R248, R400, S209, S628, S763, T247, V44, W264, W603.

Grail Romances, Vulgate B820.

<48>

Grail Sources R145.
Grail Stone Q8.
Grail Symbolism in Wolfram R59, W52.
Grail Temple P215, R270.
Grail Theme H342, L371, R315, R316, R317.
See also Sank Ryal.
Grammar C105, L390, L701, N16, N17, N18, S31, W582.
Grammar, French B690, F248, L390, T9, W582.
Grammar in Malory N11, N12, N13, N14, N15, N19, N20, N21,
N22, N23, N24.
'Grantz Geanz' B690, B692, L189.
'Grave' S618.
Greek Literature H385, M485.
Greek Origins L311.
Greek Romance B686, P363.
Green Chapel B699, C74, D37, D53, K92.
Greene, Robert M308.
Green Knight. See 'Gawain and the Green Knight'.
'Gregorius'. See Hartmann von Aue.
Grendel M94.
Grep M94.
'Grettis Saga' N254.
Griera, A. M550, R296.
Grimr The Good S508.
Grisandole P123.
Griselda G330.
Groinge Poire Mole A17.
Gruffudd, Elis J277, J279.
Gruffydd, W. J. J89.
'Gueete' M323.
Guerau de Cabrera C241.
'Guerino' K182.
'Guerrehes' S544.
Guiette, Robert P303.
Guigemar. See Marie de France.
Guilalmer R154.
Guilhem K6.
Guillaume d'Angleterre V99, W490.
'Guillaume d'Angleterre' A130, D99, F205, F255, F330, G453,
L184, O36, R99, T7, T258, W505.
See also Chretien de Troyes and Wolfram von Eschenbach.
'Guillaume de Dole' C169, H423, L718, P315, R482.
See also Jean Renart.
Guillaume de Machaut C318, H418.
'Guillaume de Palerne' D300, R482.
Guillaume de Tyr, 'Historia Belli Sacri' C59, C62.
Guillaume Le Clerc G313.
'Fergus' B693, B847, B855, E92, F479, G313, H5, J72, J313,
K148, L174, L181, L182, M158, M166, M167, M484, O100, S174,
S351, S649, S650, V36, W163.
Guilt L442.

<49>

Guinclaff E121, T237.
Guinevere   B256,   B344,   B669,   B791,   C45,   C70,   C314,   C424,
D89, D187, E17, G247, H19, H194, H658, I20, I21, I22, I23,
J221, K124, K168, K358, K374, L53, L347, L676, M25, M338, M347,
M615, N235, N253, P153, P154, P167, P203, R111, R137, R199,
S464, S473, S547, S749, S812, S894, T247, W49, W124, W164,
W231, W434, Z47.
Guinevere, False K131.
Guinevere's Guilt P153.
'Guingamor' F49, G304, H462, I12, K468, L452, M673, N132,
S544, S919, S920, W50, W113, W205, W206.
Guinganbresil N208, S579.
Guinglain B530, K364.
Guiot de Provins M591, O81A, S359, S361.
Guiot (The Scribe) F293, R128, R420.
'Guiromelant' C60, R294.
'Guiron Le Courtois' B489, B490, B501, B686, F414, F418,
L91, L92, M714, P273.
  Italian Version ('Girone il Cortese') T14.
Guivret M742.
Guorthigirn H134.
Gurnemanz W477.
Gurun M61, N9.
Guy de Dampierre T147, T149, T150.
Guy de Hostiliac B895.
Guynglaff P287.
Guyon E158.
Gwaelod B737.
Gwalchmai G192, W402, W403.
Gwenddydd E163, J277.
Gwenn E147.
Gwledig C126.
Gwrtheyrnion K184.
Gwyddeleg a' i Chwedlau W421.
Gwynedd J278, K184.
Gyburg   M322,   S371.

<50>

<51>

S464, S669, S717, V112, W52, W87, W221, W320, W341, W355, W468, W469, W480, W575, W597, W628, W633, W635, W636, W637, W666, Z101.
Hautdesert T77.
'Haveloc (Lai de)'. See 'Lai d'Haveloc'.
Hawaii L585.
Hawker, Robert Stephen, 'The Quest of the Sangraal' E19, R493.
Hebel G166.
'Hebrew Arthurian Romance, A' L42, L280, W220.
Hebrew Literature A73.
Hebrides B853.
Hector C401, K130.
Hegel, Georg Wilhelm Friedrich A84.
Heine, Heinrich B122.
Heinrich van Aken K269.
Heinrich van Veldeken, Hendrik van Veldeke F503, F504, H476, H602, J327, K330, K417, L709, M501, M502, N272, P323, S278, S435, S533, S565, T78, W632, Z79.
  'Eneit' B954, F507, T40.
  'Her Ivan' N258.
Heinrich von dem Tuerlin B193, K332, K398, R93.
  'Der Mantel' K399, W110.
  'Diu Crone', 'Diu Krone' B193, B223, B534, B561, B569, B791, C339, E6, E92, G166, G428, H302, J65, J137, J138, J139, K238, K271, K396, K397, K398, K399, L201, O16, P235, R93, R142, S136, S244, S437, S739, W68, W85, W355, W561, W654, Z70, Z76.
Heinrich von Freiburg K332, K405.
  'Tristan' B49, B176, S424, T242.
Heinrich von Ofterdingen M412.
Heinrich, Kaiser T207.
Heitstrenging E47.
'Helcanus, Roman de' N166.
Heldris de Cornualle, 'Roman de Silence' C372, G88, T143, T152, T162, T163, T164, T165, T166, T167, T168, T169.
'Heliand' S333.
Helinand B441, B442, B852.
'Hem, Roman de'. See Sarrasin, Jehan.
Hendrik van Veldeke. See Heinrich van Veldeken.
Hengist and Horsa A239, F163, H73, H662, K359, M761, R459, S267, S268, S282, V131, W104, W413.
Hengist's Watchword J272.
Henri Beauclerc, Literary Influence of his Court L186.
Henri de Blois G15.
Henry I of England E69.
Henry II of England B895, C162, G15, I11, L336.
Henry IV of England G132.
Henry VII of England G408.
Henry of Huntingdon H532, L282.
Heraldic Motifs G364, Z75.
'Her Ivan'. See Heinrich van Veldeken.

<52>

Heraldic Terms   B667.
Heraldry   B87, B622, B663, B664, D118, G76, G178, G364, H95, J4, J99, J140, K43, L445, L487, P110, P111, P258, P404, S45, S413, S491, T204.
'Herberie (Dit de l')'   M355.
Herbort von Fritzlar   A280.
Hercules   L104.
Heresy   D127, G183.
Herlekin   D78, D79.
Herman of Tournai   F24, T273.
Hermann von Thueringen   M365.
'Hermetica'   K9.
Hermetism in the Alfonsine Tradition   K8.
Hermits   B947, F122, F140, G30, J300, K117, K118, M177, M710, O103, R28, S587.
Heroes   B326, C286, C345, F412, G270, L249, P131, R14, R17, S486, S538, S539, V106, W645, W649.
 Alienated   B78.
Heroic Ideals   T126.
Heroic Tradition   T126.
Heroines   H152.
See also Women in Romances.
'Herr Ivan Lejonriddaren'   H648.
Hersart de la Villemarque   G255, G256.
 'Barzaz-Breiz'   F9, G251, G256, H570, L705, R465, T251, V50.
'Hertig Fredrik'   N257.
Herzeloyde   H293, H359, J177, K5, W477, W596.
'Herzog Ernst'   B402.
'Hexagone Logique'   B572, G26, G27.
Hierarchy of Knighthood   G158.
Higden, Ranulph   H578.
Higgins, John   C28.
'High History of the Holy Grail'   E164.
See also 'Perlesvaus'.
Hildesheim Cathedral   M420.
Hirlanda, Saint   S181.
Hispano-Arabic Poetry   L84, N293.
'Histoire des Rois d'Angleterre'   T285.
See also Geoffrey of Monmouth.
'Histoire du Morse'   K183A.
'Historia Belli Sacri'. See Guillaume de Tyr.
'Historia Britonum'   A238, B103, B571, B757, C23, C132, D135, D293, H134, J199, J282, L566, L570, R79, R206, T226.
See also Nennius.
'Historia Danorum'   T49.
'Historia de Preliis'   C59, L137.
'Historia Meriadoci'   B833, B844, M682, M730, R34, R35.
'Historia Norwegiae'   E69.
'Historia Regum Britanniae'. See Geoffrey of Monmouth.
Historical Background   A72, B446, C289, F143, F164, F472, G272, H241, H408, J8, J187, J188, M759, M760, M761, M762, O77, P68, R16, R17, R18, S344, S477, S702, S775, S817, S821, S822,

<53>

S827, S851, S852, S943, W109.
Historical Criticism A58.
Historical Triads B735.
Historical Writing H134, S644.
'Histories of Britain' E85, G16, H134, H135, J99, T285.
'Histoire du Roy Artus' W47.
History   B64,   B903,   C131,   D118,   D305,   G111,   G268,   H125,
H126, H134, H422, H584, J103, J291, L240, L260, M654, O41,
S597, S598, T227.
History of Art R312.
See also Iconography.
Hita, Archpriest of L142.
'Hiudan und Petitcreiu' G172.
Hoccleve T278.
Hoepffner, Ernest F386, I17.
Hofer, Stefan K85, R138.
Holden, Anthony John K72.
Holinshed L113.
Holmes, Ralph B636.
Holmganga L466.
Holy Blood H351, L369.
Holy Ghost O36.
Holy Grail. See Grail.
Homer B61.
Honour C448, F74, G148, M256, M262, M497, M756.
'Horn, Lay of the'. See 'Lai du Cor'.
Horn, Magic B454, B709, E73, H300, L578, S508.
Horn, King G374.
Horodisch, Abraham E143A.
Horsa. See Hengist and Horsa.
Horse's Ears F262.
Horses K44.
'Hortus Conclusus' M369.
Hospitality B834, M102.
House of Fame W321.
Hovey, Richard M25.
Hrethel The Great A222.
Huail, Son of Caw J285.
Huchoun B638.
Hue de Rotelande L145.
Hughes II de Chatillon T147, T149, T150.
Hugues d'Avalon C162.
Hughes, Thomas, 'The Misfortunes of Arthur' A247, A248,
M268, M269, R110, W69.
Hugo von Trimberg G196, R67, R526.
See also 'Renner, Der'.
Humanism F306.
Humanity B124, R58.
Humility Formula S403.
Humour E10, E11, F506, H283, K236, L366, M358, R140, R327,
R527, S471, W180.

<54>

<55>

'Ianuals Ijod' R555.
'Iarlles Y Ffynnawn' H641, H642, S393, T132.
Ibn Hazm, 'Il Collare della Colomba' (Dove's Neck-Ring)
A235A, B279, C89, G4, G48, G49, G51, L277, L278, N291.
Ibn Quzman T281.
Ibn Sina F5.
Icelandic Arthurian Material R555, T273, T274.
Icelandic Literature · B456, N4, S125, S180, S192, T53.
Icelandic Sagas   H82, K17, L432, L433, L434, L621, R500,
R501, S189, S508, S509.
Iconography A153, A192, B60, B666, B926, F15, F221, F278,
F280, F511, F534, G3, G70, H11, H199, H349, H429, H509, H658,
I28, K200, L156, L273, L472, L473, L486, L488, L492, L579,
M661, P119, R96, S147, S148, S276, S277, S342, S343, S863,
S865, S891, S892, S893, S946, S958, T104, T182, T255, V21,
W344, Y18.
See also Art, and Modena Sculpture.
Ideology B892, H645, M367, P107, R11, W544.
Idrisi B27.
Idyll M329.
'Idylls of the King'. See Tennyson.
Igerne M478.
'Ilas et Solvas' L65.
'Ille et Galeron'. See Gautier d'Arras.
Illtud, Saint B623.
Illuminated Tree W271.
Images C147, F278, L140, L317, U9.
Imitation H605, W292.
Immermann, Karl L. A142, F324, H324, K59.
 'Merlin' S149, S356, S357.
 'Tristan und Isolde' H324.
'Immram Brain' B319, M16, M17.
Immrama H84.
Incunabula P260, P263, S242.
Indian Analogues C329, C377.
Indian Origins W241, Z1.
Individuality M678, W302.
Inisfallen, Annals. See 'Annals of Innisfallen'.
Initiation F117.
Inquest B439.
Insanity in the Arthurian Romances N58.
Inscriptions M9.
Insula Avallonia or Avallonis C188, S101.
See also Glastonbury.
'Intelligenza' B254.
Inundations J170.
'Invasions, Book of' B101.
'Iosgel Isgaide Leithe' D241.
'Iphigenie' S716.
'Ipomedon' C79.
Iranian Analogues C377.
Iranian Influence R270, U11.
See also Persian Influence.

<56>

Ireland B278, C127, D161, D189, E151, H324, M7, M141, M617, M740.
Irish B286, C421, F229, G314, K380, L345, L524, M10, M300, M423, M492, R199, S100, S713, T190, Y14, Z56.
Irish Analogies C65.
Irish Arthurian Romance F10, H183.
Irish Church D110.
Irish Cycles 093.
Irish Fabulous History B794.
Irish Fairies D238.
Irish Folktales C194.
Irish Heroic Tales B786, W217.
Irish History D246, 078.
Irish Influence B788, F176, H325, H630, H667, L498, L629, M430, 075, P61, P73, P190, R41, R182, S553, S554, T175, T254, W394.
Irish Knight M307.
Irish Legend B532, D161, H179.
Irish Literature B740, B790, B883, C66, C117, C346, C423, D159, D161, D200, D235, D241, D243, D296, F13, F459, G452, H77, H493, H629, H631, J321, K364, K365, L206, L508, L509, L510, M13, M100, M281, M298, M299, M431, M741, 044, P244, S458, S463, S567, S579, T177, W419.
Irish Material L299, W307.
Irish Mythology C422, D247.
Irish Saga L539.
Irish Saints G248.
Irish School C127.
Irish Sources D163, Z54.
Irish Tradition F177, R107.
Ironsyde, Sir A22.
Irony G84, G302, G306, H31, H32, H606, H646, J28, M496, 0108, R464, U6, W670.
Is B737, 022, 023.
'Isaye le Triste' B167, G120, G121, G122, G123.
Isdernus H656, L507.
Iseo T270.
Iseult, Isold, Isolde, Isolt A207, A259, A279, B59, B153, B330, B669, B718, C145, C236, C243, C359, C454, D177, D211, D224, D269, E35, E36, E100, F8, F59, F221, F361, F362, F467, F468, F531, G3, G171, G427, G440, G451, H58, H165, H208, H268, H349, H429, H565, H566, H645, J70, J147, J213, J294, J297, J328, K47, K433, L94, L261, L265, L273, L654, M100, M161, M162, M189, M320, M422, M618, N148, N156, N157, P109, P209, P244, R72, R137, R355, R495, S307, S332, S509, S566, S594, S633, S903, S935, W296, W297, W327, W436, W620, Y11.
Iseut aux Blanches Mains, Isolt of the White Hands L467, L469, N146, R495.
See also Tristan and individual authors.
Ishtar B718, F361, M161, M162, S903.
Isis F142.
Islam 1645, M758, P366, P367.

<57>

<58>

Jacques d'Armagnac P256, P264, S413.
Jakob Pueterich von Reichertshausen, 'Ehrenbrief' R302.
Jamar, Michel M216.
James I of Scotland L566.
Jamyn, Amadis C24.
Janus D62, H662.
Japanese Literature E146, O43.
'Jaufre'   B154, B694, B695, B696, B697, B872, B873, B874,
G129, I38, J110, J117, J325, L109, L219, L223, L224, L305,
L307, L308, L366, N77, P295, P296, P371, R150, R151, R152,
R154, R155, R156, R157, R160, R285, R288, S417, S649, S650,
W144.
See also Giglan.
Jealous Husband M443.
'Jean de Paris' M712.
Jean d'Outremeuse J153.
Jean (architect). See Fenice.
Jean Renart B182, B217, C399, K281, L217, W382.
See also 'Escoufle', 'Galeran de Bretagne', 'Guillaume de
Dole', 'Lai de L'Ombre'.
Jean Sans Terre G15.
'Jeaste of Syr Gawayne' A26, B264.
'Jeeste van Walewein en het Schaakbord (De)' E138.
Jehan F206.
Jehan II d'Avesnes T150.
'Jehan et Blonde' L718.
Jehanete S722.
Jeschute Episode W477.
Jesse, Tree of B643.
Jester W195.
'Jeu de la Feuillee' P337.
Jeu Parti R158, R159.
Joachim de Flore A172, B324, B911, F191, F192, L612, O89.
Joc Grossier G314.
'Johan uz dem Virgiere' P401, S280.
Johann von Konstanz, 'Die Minnelehre' S952, W71.
Johann von Wuerzburg B196, F475, M275.
John, King of England D176, D177.
John of Glastonbury D177.
John of Salisbury, 'Policraticus' C358.
John Jones of Llynwene B102.
John Massey of Cotton, Cheshire P216.
John of Whithamstede K51, K52.
John The Baptist L344, R366.
John The Evangelist D18.
Joie d'Amour B247.
'Joie de la Cort' D95, G454, M369, P237, S207, T45, V76.
See also Chretien, 'Erec'.
Jois B163, D129.
Jones, David B401.
Jones, T. Gwynn P97, V109.

<59>

Jongleurs R502.
'Jose de Arimateia' M175, M179, M181.
'Joseph and Merlin' B838.
'Joseph d'Arimathie, Lai de'. See 'Lai de Joseph d'Arimathie'.
'Joseph of Arimathea' B82, B173, B544, B545, B629, B811,
C2, D201, F127, G77, H607, K245, K336, L23, L24, L28, L329,
L396, L566, L573, M470, M720, M743, N180, N181, N227, O4, O31,
O103, P286, R369, S543, S868, T247, V91, W514.
See also Robert de Boron.
'Joseph of Arimathea, The Portuguese Book of' B484, C80.
Joseph of Glastonbury, Saint L24.
Josephus P62.
Josso, C. P. B208.
'Joufroi de Poitiers' G339.
Jovens D128.
Juan de Flores M247, W62.
Judaism F415, S306.
'Juengere Titurel, Der'. See Albrecht von Scharfenberg.
'Juengeres Hildebrandslied' B402.
'Julian the Hospitaller' S949.
Julius Caesar F187, N61, N62.
Junkbloet W4.
Jutish Invasion W17.

<60>

Kaer-Is B737.
Kafka M39.
Kaherdin B149, N135, R355, W550.
Kaiserchronik H295.
Kalogreant. See Calogrenant
Karados H301.
'Karel Ende Elegast' H255, H261, H262.
Karg-Gasterstaedt, Elisabeth F85A.
Karrioz M532.
Katone, La L55.
Kaw of Pictland J187.
Kay, Keu A228, F17, F333, G260, H341, H606, J32, J221, J251, N237, P111, R87, S474, W204, W434, W469.
Keats, John, 'The Eve of St. Agnes' S1.
Kelliwic H318, J189.
Kenelm, Saint B795.
Kendon, Frank M659.
Kentigern, Saint B265.
Keridwen M137.
Kerrin W436.
Keu. See Kay.
Kidwelly S829.
Kilmarth Q3.
'Kilwch en Olwen' H353.
See also Kulhwych.
King and Goddess (Theme of) M11, M12.
King Arthur. See Arthur.
King Horn. See Horn, King.
'King Hrolf's Saga' J236.
King Lear. See Lear, King.
'King of Tars' H561, H562.
'King with the Corpse, The' Z58.
King's Household B35.
'King's Mirror' Y14.
Kingrimursel (Langraf) M590.
'Kings and Captains' M636.
'Kings, Beasts and Heroes' J236.
Kingship K121, M43.
Kiot. See Kyot.
Kittredge, G. L., Writings of T140.
Klingsor Z48.
Knevett, Ralph, 'Supplement of The Faery Queene' (edition) L110.
Knight E133, M266, M321, M634, P8A, R179.
 Unknightly Conduct E17.
Knight Errant. See Chevalier Errant.
'Knight of the Cart'. See Chretien de Troyes, 'Lancelot'.
'Knight of the Lion'. See Chretien de Troyes, 'Yvain'.
Knight Prisoner A128, H407.
'Knight with two   Swords'. See Balain, 'Chevalier aus deus

Espees', and Malory.
Knighthood B721, G158.
Knightly Ceremonies A14, S426, S427.
Knightly Guilt W52.
Knightly Ideal. See Chivalric Ideals.
'Knights of The Round Table' L454, S632.
Konomor M100, M144, W28.
Konrad von Wuerzburg B959, H43, K187, M413, R70.
 'Der Schwanritter' F480, K424, S284.
Krater and The Grail K7, W603.
Krimhild W48.
'Krone, Diu'. See Heinrich von dem Tuerlin.
Kuerenberc, Kuerenberg, von B602, N260.
'Kulhwch/Culhwch ac   Olwen'   B98,   C137,   D164, F30,   F227,
F228, F229, F230, F232, G189, G395, H85, H667, J36, J195, J234,
J235, J251, J254, J264, J265, J267, J268, J282, J285, J287,
L121, L412, M41, M231, O75, O104, R108, R203, R206, R350, S646,
T108, W129, W130, W241.
Kundrie A11, G198, G413, J168, P326, S288.
'Kundrunepos' R441.
Kurvenal K189, W250.
'Kymru Ne Cronigl Kymraeg' L330.
'Kyng Alisaunder' W72.
Kyot B189, D75, F14, F282, F293, F294, H24, H25, H207, H278,
K2, K4, K5, K6, K8, K9,K312, K425, M591, R248, R459, S253, S261,
S289, S302, Z40, Z41, Z43.

<62>

La Chevre W388.
Lachmann, Karl B467A, C85, H482, S678.
Lady and King, Theme of B679.
Lady of the Fountain A4, M663, S100, S665, S667, S815, T134, Z29, Z32.
See also Chretien, 'Yvain'; 'Chwedyl Iarlles y Ffynnawn'; and 'Owein'.
Lady of the Lake C56, C177, G286, G356, H499, P198.
Laehelin and the Grail Horses J170.
'Lai' (Definitions of) B143.
Lai (Literary Genre) C298, D87, M74, M203, M204, M206.
Lai (Problems and Structure of) F440, G436, M76, P248.
'Lai de Desire' G345, G436, H463, L653, M673.
'Lai de Doon' G436.
'Lai de Graelent' F49, F434, G345, H440, I12, M532, N132, S428, S429, S880, T60.
'Lai de Joseph d'Arimathie' M203.
'Lai de Lanval' B432, B530, B896, F144, F329, M388, M673, N132, P396, S417, S880, T60, T218, W368.
See also Marie de France.
'Lai de l'Espine' G436, J137, L545, W50.
'Lai de l'Ombre' P315, S70, S355, W317.
See also Jean Renart.
'Lai de Nabaret' G436, L469.
'Lai de Noton' M611.
'Lai de Plors' M203.
'Lai de Tydorel' F434, F440, G436, H388, K353, K356, L452, O25, R74.
'Lai de Tyolet' H67.
'Lai d'Haveloc' D216, G436.
See also Gaimar, Geffrei.
'Lai du Cor' B152, B238, B263, E116, H460, N295, S293, S617, T212.
'Lai du Trot' G344.
'Lai Mabon' B896.
Lai Narratif G90, J305.
'Laikibrait' C376.
Lailoken J79.
Lais, Lays A62, A92A, B1, B57, B115, B142, B144, B309, B470, B691, B920, C457, D116, D216, E7, E17, E174, F239, F403, G123, G235, G436, H159, H193, H426, H432, H433, H446, H463, H467, J161, K159, L268, L479, L720, M71, M72, M75, M220, M483, M672, N91, P185, P197, R176, R249, S160, S234, S431, S506, S726, S882, S919, S920, T198, T208, T209, W228, W533, W602, W650.
See also Breton Lais, Marie de France and other individual authors and titles.
Lakatoue L55.
Lambert d'Ardres H527.
'Lambewell, Sir' A22.
Lambrock W372.

<63>

Laments L198, R229.
Lamorat B405.
'Lancalot' (Catalan) B522, R289.
Lance, Arthur's. See Ron.
Lance, Bleeding B776, L482, L483, M423, N222, R240, R286.
Lance, Holy B884, J197, K83, N202, N220.
Lance of Longinus F415, H82, L481, L482, L483, P174.
Lance of St. Mauricius L481.
'Lanceloet en het Hert met de witte Voet' D259, H5, H67.
Lancelot A60, A201, A233, B195, B256, B265, B364, B405,
B736, C183, C358, C424, D39, D109, D259, D285, D298, E13, F106,
F259, F260, F498, G71, G284, G334, H385, H492, J2, J295, K97,
K99, K119, K231, K278, K358, K395, L205, L358, L496, L535,
L537, L542, L597, L599, L609, L610, L620, L665, L676, L681,
L682, M25, M209, M377, M462, M547, M554, M723, N184, N192,
N203, P22, P53, P128, P158, P229, P378, R143, R238, R396, S60,
S210, S332, S483, S648, T261, W512, W529, W557.
See also Chretien de Troyes, Tennyson, and Ulrich von
Zatzikhoven.
'Lancelot', French Prose A288, B73, B179, B384, B477, B493,
B494, B504, B610, B612, B613, B614, B664, B674, B713, B821,
B831, B880, B881, C35, C53, C56, C57, C70, C162, C164, C226,
C378, D20, D223, D252, F192, F368, F383, F409, F437, G245,
H194, H256, H378, H616, H657, H660, J65, J71, K130, K131, K132,
K133, K134, K135, K136, K137, K154, K273, L58, L595, L603,
L606, L608, L612, L721, M203, M205, M364, M449, M459, M461,
M462, M463, M464, M465, M466, M468, M473, N185, P158, P255,
P256, P270, R134, R264, R496, R541, S242, S417, S630, S637,
S803, S891, S892, S893, S917, T195, T197, V68, V73, V76, W47,
W162, W198, W256, W525, W659, Y7, Z60, Z92.
'Lancelot', German Prose H659, K232, K233, K234, K407, M549,
P208, R496, R497, S271, S637, S801, S802, S803, V125.
'Lancelot', Middle Dutch B265, D239, D250, D251, D252, E81,
F521, G110, G112, J309, J320, M418, N273, T194, V33, V129,
V130.
'Lancelot', Modern French Version B610, B611, B612, B613,
S592.
'Lancelot', Modern Spanish Version G54.
'Lancelot-Compilation' H1, W4.
'Lancelot-Graal' B867, F373, G22, L59, L169, M366, M460,
M572, P3, P4, P144, P153, P154, P155, P156, S779, T213, Z92.
'Lancelot of the Laik' A233, H590, S146, S542, V117.
'Saga Primitive de Lancelot du Lac' M144.
'Lancelot's Dream' J301.
Lancelot's Messianic Role F310, O106.
'Land beneath the Waves' B777.
Land's End D197.
'Landevale, Sir' L707, W368.
Landillotto C12.
Landscape S157.
Langland, William F151, H91.

<64>

Language   B51,   C411,   H333,   M128,   R312,   R503,   S12,   S324,
S325, S480, S724, S939,   S940,   S941,   V113,   W190,   W572,   W594,
W633, Z26, Z94.
'Lannoy, Les Fragments de'   J158.
'Lanseloet van Denemerken'   (Middle Dutch Drama) D287, K48,
M504, R386.
Lantien, Lantyan D178, H320, M99, M100.
'Lantsloot van der Haghedochte' H256, H260, H261, H262.
'Lanval'. See 'Lai de Lanval'
'Lanzarote' B513, B515, P284, P286.
'Lanzelet'. See Ulrich von Zatzikoven.
'Laodamia and Protesilaus' S100.
Laon Canons T20, T273.
Lapis or Lapsit Exillis D5, K354, P327, T39.
See also Wolfram von Eschenbach.
Latimarue B894.
'Latimer' B894, H165.
Latin Chronicles G115, K51, K52.
Latin Literary Tradition J92, J111.
Latin Literature, Medieval B833, C449, C451, C452, F19,
L557, M82, M107, R2, R3, U8, V103, W663, Z90.
Latin Sources C8, F18.
Laudine G139, K99, P167, P402, S661, S661A, S716.
See also Chretien, 'Yvain'.
Laughter A285, J216, M358, S65, S942, T32.
Launfal E17, H396.
'Launfal, Sir'. See Chestre, Thomas.
Laurence, Saint L670.
'Laurin' A47, A124, T141, T143, T161.
Lawman, Layamon A254, B135, B406, B417, B418, B419, B420,
B422, B424, B425, B426, B428, B459, B914, D33, D149, D203,
E175, F166, F198, F474, G282, H20, H188, H246, H608, I24, I124,
L290, L511, L582, M46, M221, M325, M691, M692, O4, P292, P386,
R121, R354, S578, S581, S642, S847, S899, S937, T15, T16, T18,
T33, T62, T69, V108, W360, W361, W513, W675, W676.
 'Brut' B283, B394, B428, B761, B762, B780, B825, C437, D207,
G149, H12, H48, H246, H247, H249, H391, K67, L363, L558, M49,
M419, P291, R140, R229, R269, R310, S166, S418, S534, S756,
S761, S762, W672.
'Lay of Emare' M534.
'Lay of the Big Fool' M299.
'Lay of the Horn'. See 'Lai du Cor'.
'Lay of the Mantel', ('Mantel Mautaille') B152, B263, B869,
H460, H469, N295, T212, U12.
Lays. See Lais, Lays.
'Le Freine' (Middle English) H397.
See also Marie de France.
Le Grand d'Aussy J48, W511.
'Leabhar Meig Shamhradhain' M37.
Lear, King C161, C249, F148, G321, H110, L111, L112,
L113, S152, S580, Z1.
'Lebor Bretnoch' D293, H77.

<65>

'Lebor Gabala' M10.
Lecto, Letto K183, P405.
Leeds J12.
Legal Customs in Tristan Legend   B410, C303, C305, F407,
R122, Y11.
Legal Procedure in the Middle Ages   B439, F329, K169, P192,
Y7, Y8, Y12.
Legend. See Myth, Mythology.
'Leges Anglorum Londoniis Collectae'   M718.
'Leges Monmutinae' P10.
'Leinster, Book of' B320, B321.
Lejeune, Rita F303.
Leland, John A233.
 'Assertio Inclytissimi Arturi' M315.
Lemaitre, Jules T249.
Leodogran G285.
Leon K144.
'Leonis, Don Tristan de'. See Tristan (Spanish).
Leonois, Lyonesse B27, B380, B845, C392, D16, M402, W487.
Leprosy C350, R150.
Levy, R. T186.
Lewis, C. S. I29, L115, M619, M622, M625, S484, W667.
Lewis, John of Llynwene G335.
Lewis, Saunders J209, L340.
'Lex et Gratia' S381.
'Li Fatti di Spagna' V100.
Lia Fail N223.
Libanor T150.
'Libeaus Desconus'. See Renaud de Beaujeau and Fair Unkown.
'Liber Floridus' D135.
'Liber Landavensis' W131.
Liberation K27.
Libraries P263, R254, S380.
See also Manuscripts and individual libraries.
'Libro de Alexandre' M479.
'Libro de Buen Amor' B4, C89, L142, M81, R517.
'Libro de las Estrellas Fixas' K8.
'Libro del Cavallero Zifar' D314, P275.
Libros de Caballerias R518.
'Libros de las Generactiones' J247.
'Life of the Black Prince' F135.
Light B576, F440, L717, R192, R193.
Linguistic Consciousness H384.
Linguistics   B196, C336, D46, F504, G38, G163, H548, K98,
L319, L373, L374, P374, R29, R200, R354, R365, S847, S932,
S939, S940, S941, T189.
Lion H160, R558.
Lion and the Serpent J182.
'Lion de Bourges, La Chanson de' K162.
Lion, Grateful B722.
Literary Art A98, B256, B270, B280, B398, C90, C215, C283,

<66>

C286, C298, D114, D225, F57, F407, F413, F481, G13, G14, G19, G189, G379, H37, H219, H294, H555, H568, H581, H634, J38, J39, J43, K101, K273, K282, L16, L366, L378, L388, L397, L432, L448, L718, L719, L725, M366, M565, M632, M633, M688, M753, O54, O55, P12, P151, P248, R85, R245, R497, R534, R535, R557, S123, S255, S496, S497, S663, S742, S743, S785, S799, S908, V72, V103, W96, W231, W473.

Literary Criticism A58, B392, C208, D101, F391, F484, H578, K208, L304, M312, M650, M707, S692, T89.

Literary History B323, G43, K306, P159, P387.

Literary Interpretation G435, L164.

Literary Life B13, C277, S408.

Literary Portraiture B398, B409, C208, L432, L434, M165.

Literary Terminology R312, R357.

Literary Theory G168.

Literature and Fine Arts F56.

Literature and Society C169, L671, M363, M478.

Lithuania P405.

Little Britain W653.
See also 'Arthur of Little Britain'.

Liturgy K212, Q2, T39, W571.

Liver Sea L263.

Livingston, Charles H. M88.

'Livre d'Artus' F483, G18, K135, K181, K182, S629, S630, W50, W220, W316, W385.

'Livre d'Isis' K7.

'Livre de Blaise, Fragments du' R477.

Llandaff B763, P287.

'Llen Cymru' L402.

'Lloegr' B102, J122, J123.

'Lludd and Llevelis', 'Llud and Llevelys' A5, B756, C187, R345, S823, V107.

Llwyd, Humphrey W393.

Llwyfenydd H495.

'Llyfr Coch O Hergest'. See 'Red Book of Hergest'.

'Llyfr Gwyn'. See 'White Book of Rhydderch'

Llywarch Hen B743, H357, J284.

Llywarch The Aged J6, W402, W403.

Loathly Bride C332.

Loathly Lady A99, L286.

'Locus Amoenus' C147, H165, T171.

Loeseth B483.
See also Tristan.

Logres B102, J123.

Lohengrin A259, B941, C382, D221, F173, F480, G228, H651, K420, K425, L52, P341, R504, S210, S228, S374, T96, V5, W230, W233.
See also Konrad von Wuerzburg, Swan Knight, and Wagner.

Loherinc, The Legend of R247.

Lohot B822, H616A.

London B422, N61.

London Colloquium F453.

<67>

Longes Mac N-Uislenn H632.
Longinus, Lance of. See Lance.
Loomis, Laura Hibbard N144.
Lope de Vega P39.
Lost Literature of Medieval England W535.
Lot, Ferdinand B595, L607.
Lot, King L622, M631.
Lot-Borodine, Myrrha M456.
Loth B98.
Louis d'Anjou C60.
Loup-Garou G436.
See also Werewolf.
Love F423, J41, K109, Q7.
Love and Melancholy K164.
Love and Order in the Medieval German Courtly Epic W481.
Love and the Meaning and Uses of 'Amors' F416.
Love, Conception of D38.
Love Conventions B702, R359.
Love, Courtly. See Courtly Love.
Love Debate B156, B593, B954, E25.
Love, Human B644, C231, C345, C445, G437, S371.
Love, Illicit H645, T5.
Love in Medieval Romances G161, K338, P355, W167.
Love in the 'Romans d'Antiquite' J255.
Love Potion B329, C10, C101, C445, F59, F407, G41, H645,
J157, L465, S307, T270, V53.
Love, Profane L618.
Love, Sacred L618.
Love Service L376.
Love, Virtuous J333.
Love, Western B917, R481.
Lovelich, Henry A16, B639.
 'Merlin' A15, K277, R64.
Lovers' Grotto D169, G148, H165, H229, J38, J53, K310, O8,
P347, R49, R72, W88.
Lucan C412, M268.
Lucca H351.
Luces de Gast S842.
See also 'Tristan', French Prose.
Lucius W529.
Ludgate H572.
Ludwig II of Bavaria K268, T96.
Luf-Lace H368.
Lug E172, G329, K379, L537.
Lugh Lamhfhada O15.
Luigi Alamanni H235.
Lull, Ramon A119, D139.
Lunete G139, P167, S27, S53, S378, S716.
Lydgate, 'Complaint of the Black Knight' P173.
Lyonesse. See Leonois.
Lyric Genres I11.

<68>

<69>

'Mabinogion' A4, A5, A6, A7, B51, B56, B245, B399, B447, B535, B536, B537, B886, C59, C122, C157, D36, D164, E76, E77, E79, E147, E148, E155, E165, F219, F230, F231, F328, G39, G134, G186, G187, G189, G394, G396, G397, G398, G399, H128, H209, I6, I7, J24, J89, J102, J180, J230, J231, J233, J235, J238, J244, J251, J252, J254, J265, J281, J285, L70, L335, L336, L338, L343, L347, L535, L626, L627, L633, L641, L668, M13, M18, M281, M668, M702, N285, R107, R108, R188, R200, R201, R308, R339, R442, S100, S364, S646, S666, S815, S816, T69, T131, T133, T134, V28, V49, W10, W48, W103, W130, W132, W398, W402, W403, W405, W413, W446, W665, Z32, Z35.
Mabon G87.
'Mabon' B896.
Mabon vab Modron G395.
Mabonagrain B374, P355, S61.
Maboroshi-no-Tate O43.
Machiavelli P391.
Madness D219, H576.
'Madoc' C183.
Madoc, Prince A265.
Madog J98.
Mador K128.
Maen Huail J285.
'Maerlent et Boendale' C240.
Maelgwn J278.
'Magauran, Book of' M37.
Magic D243, G267, M279.
Magic Horn. See Horn, Magic.
Magical Kingdom M266.
Magical Tests T53.
Magician W45, Z89.
Magnus Maximus P68, S852, W28, W29.
Magus B956.
Maiden with Golden Hair G219.
Maimed Kings F189, M329, O88, R264.
Maister Massy T278.
Maligne T143.
Malory, Sir Thomas A25, A51, A128, A174, A204, A205, A233, A252, A273, A287, B35, B90, B90A, B109, B121, B259, B266A, B272, B635, B641B, B641A, B700, B703, B914, C134, C140, C217, C326, D38, D39, D40, D41, D145, D209, D210, D225, D274, D276, E21, E129, E130, F62, F64, F106, F107, F110, F111, F113, F115, F116, F137, F319, G7, G81, G233, G239, G301, G333, H296, H303, H304, H367, H407, H507, H634, H670, H671, H672, J131, J247, J312, K45, K92, K122, K123, K125, K126, K128, K141, K143, K147, K196, L35, L87, L129, L288, L313, L520, L642, L676, L683, L687, M239, M240, M241, M282, M284, M285, M307, M510, M518, M620, M626, M677, M691, M711, M726, N152, N168, N169, N170, N233, N242, N243, N244, N271, O49, O91, O108, P104, P224, P242, R91, R92, R121, R143, R198, R261, R278, R374, R523, S5, S12, S472, S474, S501, S597, S857, S898, T3, T68, T69, T81, T138,

<70>

T198, V52, V54, V55, V60, V61, V63, V70, V90, V122, V124, W66,
W67, W78, W332, W361, W364, W516, W517, W518, W519, W520, W521,
W522, W523, W524, W525, W529, W530, W531, W532, Y3, Y10.
  'Arthuriad' K248, K249.
  'Book of Balin' F107, K105, L474, L580, M208, R212, R524,
V41, V85.
  'Book of Gareth' D212, G283, G419, M171.
  'Fair Maid of Astolat' R261.
  'Morte Darthur' A22, A25, A162, A195, A196, A205, A221,
A256, A286, B134, B256, B272, B273, B293A, B391, B392, B579,
B580, B641A, B641B, B689, B703, B705, B815, C139, C363, C379,
C409, D42, D45, D71, D158, D225, D298, E146, F106, F109, F112,
F118, F121, F498, F499, F500, G158, G175, G209, G299, G332,
G415, G417, G418, H185, H402, H498, H499, H577, J332, J333,
K103, K104, K121, K124, K128, K141, K170, K171, K248, K270,
K463, L36, L80, L551, L678, L679, L680, L681, L682, L684, L686,
M96, M97, M98, M148, M242, M280, M283, M313, M554, M616, M627,
M628, M631, M632, M633, M664, M698, M724, M725, N16, N17, N18,
N68, O6, O49, O64, O111, P131, P332, R187, R211, R519, R524,
S12, S48, S207, S215, S332, S379, S446, S473, S475, S503, S637,
S638, S811, S861, S862, S897, T266, T267, T271, U13, V58, V59,
V80, V82, V122, W66, W67, W136, W287, W288, W289, W304, W512,
W515, W526, W527, W668, W669, Y12.
  'Selected Tales' B5, V83, V85, V86.
  'Tale of the Sankgreal' H670, H672, W334.
  'Works' E21, N11, N12, N13, N14, N15, N19, N20, N21, N22,
N23, N24, R521, V80, V81, V83, V84, V87.
'Manawyddan' L335, M18, S508.
Mandeville's 'Travels' L539.
Manessier B861, I40.
Manicheans A171.
'Manon Lescaut' H647.
Manorbier W32.
Mantel E93.
'Mantel, Lay of the', 'Mantel Mautaille'. See 'Lay of the
Mantel'.
'Manuel et Amande' Z67.
Manuscript Illumination G71, L579, S891, S892, S893, Y18.
Manuscript Tradition M555.
Manuscripts B57, B82, B244, B256, B486, B487, B488, B489,
B510, B676, B685, B942, C168, C304, C441, C443, E20, E53, F31,
F457, G66, G132, G178, G239, G337, H106, H115, H168, H595, J2,
J80, J105, J212, J281, K74, K142, K410, L143, L361, L378, L379,
L380, M108, M296, M382, M434, M462, M463, M464, M466, M606,
M662, M715, N30, N31, N238, O28, O29, O34, P51, P263, P383,
R300, R313, R365, R420, S122, S151, S238, S243, T104, T165,
U18, V63, W393, W437, W577, W609, Y4.
See also Facsimiles.
  'Amsterdam' C182.
  'Annonay' P142.
  'Auchinleck' B430, E21, K110, L360, M44.
  'Berlin' E73.

<71>

'Berne' P395, R355.
'B. N. Fr. 594' F48.
'Bodmer' B508.
'Brogyntyn' J213.
'Cambridge' R355, T285.
'Chetham' H509.
'Cologne: W. Folio' K154, K202.
'Copenhagen' S541.
'Cotton Cleopatra BV' P91, W393.
'Cotton Nero AX' G207, H386, P395.
'Danish' R1.
'Dublin 23, N.10' B319.
'Dublin, Trinity College' H115.
'Durham C IV XXVII.I' N155.
'Exeter' B261, H113, J261.
'Folger VA 139' M64.
'French' B472, B473, B676, C441, S30.
'Geneva' B508, L92.
'German Libraries' B658.
'Giessen' M572.
'Guiot' F48, F358, R421, R436.
'Heidelberg' F280, K231, W609.
'Heralds College' L454.
'Historia' H119.
'Iolo' L347.
'Ireland' D148, I27.
'Lankowitz' H486.
'Latin' B351.
'Laval-Middleton Ms.' C372.
'Liege, Val St. Lambert' A10.
'Lincoln' (Ms. Thornton) B706.
'Llanstephan' R331, W659.
'Loccum, Klosterbibliothek' B194, D264.
'London, British Library' (Harley 2252) B832.
'London Grays Inn' (Ms. 7) M719.
'Madrid' P282, P283.
'Manchester' P255.
'Modena' R324.
'Morbihan' B483.
'Munich, Cod. Germ.' G127, H374, U12.
'New York' B509.
'Nottingham' A124, C370, T168.
'Ottobonianus' F172.
'Oxford' (Bodleian Library) B510, C299, M745.
'Oxford' (Douce) B510, E21, H129, M44, T168.
'Oxford' (Jesus College) P384, R205.
'Panton' R331, S25.
'Paris' (Bibliotheque du Roi) P51.
'Paris B. N.' B200, N155, P134, P261, S621, S624, S628.
'Pierpont Morgan Library' B492, R331.
'Peniarth' B735.

<72>

'Red Book' J238, R201.
'Rennes' (B. Mun.) Z72.
'Rylands' P255.
'Tristan en prose' M181.
'Vatican Grail' O28.
'Venice' (St. Mark's) B549.
'Vienna' F104, M382, U12.
'Vulgate' T104.
'Welsh' B100, B244, J252, N30.
'White Book' J238, J262, J264.
'Wigmore' G131.
'Winchester' A195, A205, A221, B90A, H303, H304, K141, K143, M98, O6, S48, S49, S503, V59, V63, V80, V87, V124, Y3.
'Zadar' N155.
Manx Folklore R186.
Map, Walter B66, B266, B619, C162, M168, P241, W108, W162.
'De Nugis' D29, H392, L512.
'Mar' C105.
Marc, King. See Mark, King.
Marcabru E127, R360.
March N148.
March ap Meirchion J242.
Marcus Quonomorius C129.
'Mare Amoroso' G56.
Margaret, Saint A146, R120.
Marginalia F199.
'Mariaen' J309.
'Marie, Abbess of Shaftesbury' B895, F316.
Marie de Champagne B275, F310, L230, S760, V95.
Marie de France, 'Lais' A62, A93, A123, B57, B120, B142, B164, B199A, B305, B379, B716, B717, B745, B765, B836, B849, C269, C355, C457, D13, D28, D73, D87, D88, D111, D112, E184, F65, F156, F178, F179, F238, F239, F241, F242, F243, F256, F258, F315, F317, F329, F332, F355, F417, F481, F516, G250, G271, G311, G345, H157, H388, H419, H422, H423, H424, H425, H426, H430, H431, H434, H435, H436, H443, H467, H522, H524, H526, H640, I11, J155, J306, K239, K455, L39, L107, L122, L153, L164, L181, L228, L242, L246, L267, L269, L270, L271, L272, L274, L291, L292, L382, L430, M100, M220, M494, M496, M498, M499, N8, N9, N93, O52, P180, R176, R181, R249, R255, R271, R273, R274, R287, R356, R359, R381, R416, R470, R472, R482, R556, S26, S117, S160, S208, S234, S235, S283, S339, S430, S431, S492, S618, S725, S726, S728, S731, S779, S853, T54, T61, T62, T268, T286, V4, W74, W112, W113, W124, W125, W228, W286, W308, W367, W390, W487, W544, W554, W604, W650, Z91.
See also Lais.
'Bisclaveret' B48, B118, C186, I11, L631, M494, R471, W112.
'Chaitivel' G311, I11, M494.
'Chevrefeuille, Chevrefoil, Chevrefueil' A44, B572, C9, D96, D309, F334, F355, F392, H193, H432, H459, I11, J152, K24, L164, M72, M100, M172, M494, M747, N249, O97, P20, P165, R191, S75,

<73>

<74>

F152, H532, J36, J226, K218, K439, K447, K449, L18, L128, L169, L395, L471, L485, L668, M243, M616, M621, P253, P313, R5, R372, S222, S686, S794, S854, T89, T130, T218, T219, W77, W182, W634, Z38.
  Studies G43.
Medieval Society W142.
Medievalists L4.
'Meic Gartnain' B359.
Meisterlied E73.
Melanges. See Festschriften.
Meleagant C314, S480.
'Meliacin' S27.
'Meliador'. See Froissart.
'Meliadus' L91, W358.
'Melior' V56.
Melissa I25.
Meljanz M583.
'Melora Agus Orlando'. See 'Orlando Agus Melora'.
'Melusine Maternelle Et Defricheuse' L190, L191.
Melwas J221, W434.
Menhir D277.
'Meraugis de Portlesguez'. See Raoul de Houdenc.
Merfyn Frych K184.
Mergell, Bodo B360, R508, R528.
Meriadoc B833, M682.
'Merlijn' (Dutch) H254.
Merlin A15, A73, A264, B70, B225, B293, B324, B364, B384, B476, B485, B497, B516, B529, B755, B793, B837, B956, C5, C25, C50, C121, C142, C221, C222, C285, C388, D34, E120, E161, E162, F217, F320, F324, F326, F347, F487, F517, G103, G151, G255, G285, H102, H107, H134, H156, H620, I25, J18, J19, J58, J94, J95, J97, J100, J101, J136, J217, K37, K128, K133, K135, K170, K245, K332, K365, K366, K371, K375, K423, L58, L97, L233, L280, L360, L535, L549, L566, L592, M5, M38, M196, M201, M209, M228, M274, M314, M733, M754, N25, N27, N39, N60, N198, O28, O114, P65, P122, P125, P238, P272, P369, P384, R275, R329, R330, R465, R524, S1, S44, S102, S149, S161, S177, S203, S242, S373, S567, S580, S821, S825, S826, S832, S837, S841, S917, T30, T31, T50, T51, T147, T150, T168, T169, V62, V85, W213, W282, W312, W325, W326, W377, W394, W397, W416, W422, Z86, Z87, Z92.
See also 'Arthour and Merlin', Emerson, Geoffrey of Monmouth, Richard of Ireland, and Robert de Boron.
  'Merlin L'Enchanteur' B611, B612, B613, B615, C223, Q5, R396.
  'Merlin Silvestris' B434.
  'Prophecies of Merlin' B73, B324, B505, B516, B857, B858, B859, C183, E23, E69, G103, J58, K182, K274, M108, N60, O28, P121, P127, P128, P272, R329, S242, S365, S417, T13.
See also Richard of Ireland.
  'Suite du Merlin' B474, B478, B479, B481, B491, B501, B511,

<75>

F78, H614, K128, M209, O28, P49, R524, S577, V62, V66, V76, W524, W528.
  'Suite Huth du Merlin' B710, M201, M454, N198, P49, S624, T149.
  'Vita Merlini'. See Geoffrey of Monmouth.
  Vulgate 'Merlin' A52, B838, D73, L57, M442, M447, M451, M455, M458, O28, P49, S623, S630.
See also Myrddin.
'Merlin', English Prose C389, S904, W653.
Merlin, Italian, 'Storia di Merlino' S50.
'Merlin', Modern French Translation S592.
Merlin's Birth D21, D22.
Merlin's Death F217.
Merlin's Island L262.
'Merlini, Prophetia' E12, E23, F171, F172, R330, R331, R341.
See also Geoffrey of Monmouth.
'Merveilles de Rigomer, Les' D275, F206, K454, P207, R536, S354, S795, S806, V37.
Mervyn, Saint D195.
Mervyn Vrych L640.
'Merwunder' L140.
Messire F249.
Mesure B920.
'Metamorfosis del Caballero' A139.
Metamorphoses J25.
'Metamorphoses' (Apuleius) K4, K7.
'Metaphors' Z50.
Metaphors, Medieval Tradition of Z51.
Metham, John P7.
Metrical Forms B357, C447, L7, P335, S278.
Metrical Romances L456.
Mezura W279.
Micheau Gonneau P264.
Middle Ages V121.
Middle Class in Romances R67.
Middle English Literature. See English Literature, Medieval.
Middle High German. See German Literature, Medieval.
Middleton, Christopher A233, M315.
Middleton Family T167.
'Miles Gloriosus' R170.
Milton, John B423, B427, F143, F164, F471, F472, G167, J249, K344, M711, M759, R121, W111, W329.
'Milun'. See Marie de France.
Mimesis A281, A282, A283, A284, C450, H358, J330, S131.
Miniatures S892, S893, T104.
Minnegrotte. See Lovers' Grotto.
'Minnelehre'. See Courtly Love, Johann von Konstanz.

<76>

Minnesang, Minnesong A145, B381, E8, E59, E114, F101, F286, F357, F502, F503, F527, I30, J310, K332, L40, L51, M173, M399, M645, M646, M647, M653, N50, O18, P351, P392, S202, S226, S658, S676, W168, W191.
Minnesingers K443, M687, S52, T57, T139.
Minstrels B137.
Mirabilia G147, R350, Y14.
Miracles L447.
'Mirror for Magistrates' C28, F37.
'Mirror of Love' M751.
Miscellany J16.
Misogyny B450, B451.
Mistral, Frederic C22.
Mithraism S810, S812.
Modena B493, L490, P376.
Modena Sculpture D89, D136, G99, H656, H658, J129, K218, K220, L244, L489, L492, L493, L494, L496, L507, L514, L517, L579, M80, N241, O60, P375, P377, S865.
Modena State Archives B495.
Modern Language Association, Arthurian Romance Section A28.
Modern Versions N191, N266.
Modred, Mordred B830, L496, L535, N234, O115, R113, R524, S11, W530.
Modron M268, N132.
'Moettuls Saga' B879, H52.
'Molaynes' S96.
Mold Library C248.
Mommsen W410.
Monasticism P233.
Monologues (Author's) D114, M565.
Monroe, Harriet L650.
Mons Agned B421.
Mons Badonicus C334.
See also Battles, Arthur's.
Monsters F482, H147, L140.
Mont Saint-Michel F133, R379, T146.
Montalvo A137, P310.
Montesinos, Cave of F517.
Monteverdi, Angelo S907.
Montsalvat, Montsalvatsch, Montserrat E152, G72, H273, H274, H275, H276, H277, P327, S225, S453, W477.
Montsegur G72.
Moorish Influence G45, G46, G47, G50, M374.
Moors in Spain L275, S34.
Morals B59, B152, B256, B947, B948, C170, G436, H389, H588, H645, L241, L242, M389, M498, M507, P161, P340, S587, S872.
Morbihan Fragment B483.
Mordavian Folklore E100, L94.
Mordrain B820.
Mordred. See Modred.

<77>

Morgain, Morgan Le Fay   B139, B496, B498, B715, C73, D217,
E1, F22, F267, F341, F342, F347, F491, H40, K181, K182, L496,
L527, L535, L560, M410, M541, M615, M664, N132, O64, P7, P337,
S670, T217, V76, V77, W49, W127, Z32.
Morgante   A86, A87, A88, A89, A91, F41, F42, G116, M131,
M132, R475, R538, S54, W356, W357.
Morholt   B374, D133, D177, M210, P243.
'Moriaen'   B960, D286, H1, H2, H3, H5, H255, H256, H257,
H258, H259, H261, H262, L153, L362, P4, P5, T79, W219, W220,
W277.
'Morien and Merlin'   T50.
Moritz von Craon   H196.
Morois, Forest of. See Morrois, Forest of.
Morold   F194.
Morolt of Ireland   L454, S654.
Morphology   R445.
Morrigu   M410.
Morris, William   D3, H492, J214, K469, L398, P203,   R121,
S749, T122, T287.
Morrois, Forest of   B644, J297, L167, N167, V74, V76, W306.
'Mort Artu' (French Prose Romance)   B343, B471, B476, B612,
B613, B614, B831, C57, C58, D141, F78, F366, F457, G182, H478,
K119, K128, L17,   L280,   M128,   M438,   M723, P193, R546, R547,
R550, S592, V46, W517, Z15.
  (Dutch Version)   G108.
'Morte Arthur'   C32, C409.
'Morte Arthur' (Stanzaic Middle English)   B274, B322, B449,
B832, D209, E146, H398, H399, M318, R121, R229, R230, T284,
W234, W517.
Morte Arthur Theme   B823, B826, B827, C328.
'Morte Arthure'   B661, F138, J166, R229, S897, Z15.
'Morte   Arthure',   Alliterative   A156,   A157,   B271,   B274,
B449, B574, B661, B706, B796, B815, B832, B933, C210, C218,
C437, E70, E146, E175, F129, F130, F131, F132, F134, F135,
F137, F138, G62, G181, G239, G323, G373, H12, H89, H249, H370,
H413, H537, H539, J46, J166, J167, K61, K62, K63, K64, K65,
K270, K335, K336, K395, K412, K413, K414, L480, L582, L685,
M237, M241, M304, M691, M692, M739, N87, O1, O2, O4, O57, O71,
P57, P369, R113, R121, R140, R197, R230, S22, S141, S142, S279,
S656, S947, S948, S948A, T234, T277, W671.
'Mort(e) Le Roi Artu'   A58, B384, B389, B437, B683, C3, F321,
F367, F416, F422, F443, F450, I13, I18, K126, L61, L82, M347,
M366, M598, M752, N234, N236, O92, P139, R396, S630, W314, Y7,
Z100.
'Morte d'Arthur'. See Tennyson.
'Morte Darthur'. See Malory.
'Morte di Tristano'   S56.
'Morte Vivante'   F187, H238.
Mosaic of Otranto   H225, H230.
Mother   G270.
Motif-Indexes   B456, C423, S192.

<78>

Mount Badon. See Badon Hill.
Moytura, Battle of S713.
Mozarabic Songs A126.
Mozarabic Spain D317.
'Mudiad Rhamant' O110.
'Mule Sanz Frain' B534, C202, H387, J185, O105, O106, O107, S568.
Munday, Anthony H243.
Muntschoye H338.
Murals. See Wall Paintings.
Music   C149, G104, G171, M72, M73, M74, M75, M76, M278, T244.
Musical Customs, Medieval M73.
Musical Instruments S786, T244.
Musical Terms T56.
Musical Versions N191.
Musil, Robert, 'Mann ohne Eigenschaften' F466.
Mutel, Rene P367.
Mynord R106.
Mynweir R106.
Myrddin C221, E150, E163, E168, J5, J18, J93, J100, J103, J104, J105, J276, J277, J279, L309, M136, R487, R488, W416, W422.
See also Merlin.
'Myrddin a Thaliesin, Ymddiddan' L323, W376.
Myrddin Emrys B680.
Myrddin Wyllt L337.
Mysticism B360, C235, F153, G154, K448.
Myth, Mythology A266, B119, B168, B373, B433, C165, D17, D217, D218, D247, F440, G24, G274, G416, H191, H405, H546, H669, J25, J145, J206, J208, J291, K239, K325, K360, K379, K381, K382, L190, M15, M279, M621, M688, O79, P25, P356, R17, S125, S446, S823, S825, S831, T249, U5, U14, V106, V132, W274, W630, Z58.
Myth of the Magus B956.
'Myvyrian Archaeology' B753.

<79>

Nadler G328.

Names, Arthurian A17, A33, B98, B841, K338, M617, N207, N224, N229, R206, R350, S452, S453, W377, W657.

Names, Index of A33, C153, F185, F201, W248.

Names, Personal B412, B818, B819, B825, B841, F229, G352, H665, W176.

Names, Place B419, B425, B799, B810, C376, D182, J13, J126, K73, L185, L545, M241, P154, P240, P309, Q3, Q4, R350, S102, S348, S810, S878, S904, T92, T269, W11, W377, W659, W659.

Names, Proper B104, B465, F284, H393, L239, L441, S358, S382, S436, W248.

See also Onomastics.

Namur (Comte de) L240.

Nanteos Cup S16.

'Narcisus' P181.

Narison (Dame de) P167.

Narrative Art A41, B291, B567, B654, H383, L359, L463, N250, R11, R261, S5.

Narrative Forms B296, C26, D225, G44, G436, L443, L453, N296, S586, S705, U4, U5, U6.

Narrative Structure in Chretien's 'Yvain' U3.

Narrative Structure in 'Floire et Blancheflor' H35.

Narrative Technique A43, B109, B168, B389, B659, B670, B716, B936, C318, C440, D295, F107, G34, G42, G189, H36, H383, H633, H642, I42, K63, K201, K343, L119, M153, M496, N240, P176, P334, P398, R19, R269, R470, R541, R559, S77, S194, T101, U6.

Narrative Tenses F234.

Narrative Themes R482.

Narrator D61, J28, K250, O108.

Nascien B819.

Nationalism K307, S222.

National Library of Wales J212, J243, S242, W437.

Nature and Art S405.

Nature in Chretien de Troyes L698.

Nature Topoi L699.

Nauclerus, Johannes F148.

Navarre E68.

Navigation M129.

Neckam, Alexander L692.

Nennius A149, A264, B248, B301, B419, B558, B723, C112, C123, C137, C393, D152, D280A, E171, F26, F30, F196, G2, G147, H77, H424, J8, J222, J266, K345, K346, K348, K350, K351, L309, L314, L356, L357, L634, L635, L637, L639, N122, N193, N196, O75, R79, R103, R121, R459, T93, T108, T178, T179, W8, W17, W18, W19, W34, W396, W401, W406, W408, W409, W410, W413, W414, Z53.

   'Historia Britonum' A238, B571, D281, D290, F26, H135, J18, K184, L21, L604, S423, T225, W14, W15.

Neo-Latin World G426.

Nerones F187.

Neutral Angels H205.

<80>

'Neveux, Les' B341.
New World C166.
Newberry Library, Chicago C293, F157, H141, U19.
Newstead, Helaine H649, M89.
Newton, Humfrey C455.
'Nghymrus, Y Stori Werin Yng' J287.
'Nibelungenlied' B180, B561, B567, C309, D283, H555, K341,
K450, L442, M394, N7, O19, O46, R379, R441, S212, S799, W48.
Nicetas Choniates C59.
Nicodemus's Gospel F214, M470, O103, O106.
Nightingale T65.
Nine Worthies H414, S290.
Niniane H127, N214, R483.
Nitze, William A. M87, R320, R321, W646.
'Nobiliario' S598.
Noble Heart M425.
'Nodons-Nuadu' B865.
Normandy B643.
Normans C346, G140, H349, H350, R502.
'Norroena Riddarsager' H52.
Norse Literature   C122, E74, G441, H108, K159, N254, P356,
S125.
Norse Motifs B424.
Norse Relations with Wales C156, G396, L338.
Norse Studies B774, T274.
Norse Versions H81, K267, R555.
Northumbria B386, C132.
Norway N297.
Notker T42.
Novel C170, C193, C239, F220, G21, G52, H165, K293, Z72.
'Novele' K96.
Numbers M657, M658, R253.
Numerical Composition C426, H601, S654.
Numerical Structures G139, H368, L381.
Numerical Patterns H369, K201.
Nun in Literature B963.
Nyme H499.
Nymia, Saint M42.

<81>

<82>

P360, P409, R37, R460, S455, T105, T217.
See also Ariosto and 'Roland Furious'.
'Orlando Innammorato'. See Boiardo.
Orosius S576.
Orpheus K186.
'Orphee et Proserpine' F432.
'Ortu Walwanii (De)' B833, D52.
'Os Cavaleiros Do Rei Artur' (Modern Portuguese Translation
of Malory) D119.
Osiris F142.
Osteilli, Sire de B895.
'Othea's Epistle to Hector' G241.
Otherworld B55, B267, B434, D172, H405, H406, J155, L706,
M15, M17, M125, O90, P112, P113, P114, P115, P232, P347, S508,
S931, V114.
Otherworld Journeys B128, F311, T130, W3.
Otherworld Motifs P113.
Otranto. See Mosaic of Otranto.
Outlandish Stranger T128.
Ovid B462, C413, G42, G446, H117, L142, P324, W490.
'Ars Amandi' O83, W353.
Owain, Owein B98, B756, B784, C184, D164, E77, F139,
F231, G191, G192, J254, L652, M18, P346, R203, R206, R343, T134,
W423.
See also 'Mabinogion'.
Owen, Robert B624.
Owen-Pughe, William J180.
'Owen and Lunet' A4, G193, S871.
'Owen's Stone' J217.
'Owl and Nightingale' G62, H619.
Oxford S24.

<83>

Pacolet D79, F408.
Padarn, Saint B623.
Paganism H165, S306.
Paien de Maisieres C202, H387, J185, S568.
'Demoisele a la Mule' O81.
Painters A211, I28.
Paintings B800, G71.
'Palach' (Welsh Arthurian Poem) L413.
Palaeography F31, G163, H241, M108.
'Palamede' B477, B481, B482, B486, B487, B488, B489, B495,
F59, L91, L93, L368, L438, L439, L440, P273.
See also Guiron le Courtois.
Palermo G3, L273.
'Palmeirim de Inglaterra', H243, H244, L77, M174, M638,
M639, P117, R478, T98.
Pandragus F190.
'Pandragus et Libanor' F190.
'Pantagruel' F343.
Panzer, Friedrich K445.
Paolo H194.
Paradise, Earthly G316.
Paraphrases C213.
'Parcevals' (Old Norse Saga) L587, M562.
Parents in Medieval Romance O98.
'Paris et Vienne' S115.
'Parise la Duchesse' B185.
'Parliament of the Three Ages' G62.
'Parmolinu d'Oliva' F327.
Parody M329.
Parry, John Jay A217, E154, L44, S915.
'Parsifal' C37, F162, S715, V5.
See also Wagner.
'Parsiwalnamae' R117, S933, S934.
Partholon H78, M679, T181.
'Parthonopeus' H253.
'Partonopeus de Blois' G143, G339, H136, M168, M289, N132,
S711.
Parzival, Perceval A71, A73, A82, A120, A167, B31, B44,
B131, B154, B270, B317, B506, B533, B861, B928, C60, C358, D1,
D153, E24, F312, F474, G15, G223, G226, G228, G288, G414, H22,
H52, H340, H345, H378, H411, H515, H544, J67, J145, J226, K32,
K34, K149, K216, K219, K278, L279, L298, L353, L535, M253,
M318, M331, M405, M545, N131, N132, N218, N246, O101, P8A, P46,
P138, R42, R257, R293, R324, R393, S25, S28, S143, S209, S221,
S225, S285, S347, S360, S625, S763, S869, S917, T218, T261,
W38, W156, W262, W272, W276, W610, W648, Z48, Z98.
(Alsatian) H299, H301.
(Early English Metrical) H56.
(French Prose) F405, P138.
See also Chretien, 'Mabinogion', Ulrich Fueetrer, and
Wolfram.

<84>

Parzival Paintings B926, S276, S277.
Parzival Problems S221, W81.
Parzival Question W52.
Parzival Fragment E49.
Parzival, Son of C382.
Parzival's Guilt D168, M253, W52.
Parzival's Struggles F80.
Pascent A239.
Passage Perilleux L652.
Passion of Christ L266.
'Patience' C99, K333, L156, S534, S691, W508, Z24.
Patrick, Saint B358, C68, H121, H134, L259, M125, S844.
Patronage, Literary B275, K299, L180, M295, P264, S760.
Paul de Leon, Saint A278, C129, K144.
Pauphilet, Albert F383.
Paving Tiles H11, L486.
Peacock, Thomas Love W664.
'Pearl' A2, B378, B404, C99, C212, E94, F35, H368, K333,
L156, L696, P216, P395, S534, S691, T223, T278, W508.
Peasants B26, M519, R67.
'Pecol/Quelpol' F408.
'Pedair Cainc y Mabinogi' J102.
Pelee, La Legende De' S384.
'Pelerinage de Charlemagne' C420, L475, S178, W73, W76.
Pellean B818.
'Pelleas and Ettard' V85.
Pelles B818, C52, M642, N186, R286, S474, S701.
Pellinor, Pellynor B481, B818, D41, M631, R524.
Pembrokeshire L336.
Pendragon D93, J85, L636, L643, M478, P68, S11, T150.
Pentangle H368.
'Perceforest',   'Perceforet'   F181, F182, F183, F186, F187,
F188, F189, K181, K182, L332, L421, L429, M480, S8, S722, S917,
T51.
Perceval. See Parzival, Perceval.   See also Chretien de
Troyes, 'Didot-Perceval',   'Peredur', 'Perlesvaus', Schaeffer,
Wolfram von Eschenbach.
'Perceval of Galles, Sir' B44, B79, C30, E11, G29, H544.
'Perchen Machreu' J91.
'Perchevael', Middle Dutch D248, F521, Z23.
'Percheval li Gallois' R376.
'Percivals Saga' (Norse) F213.
Percy, Thomas D120, D122.
Percy's Folio Manuscript F490, W452.
Percy's 'Reliques' F489.
Percyvale, Sir M510.
'Percyvelle, Sir' B785, F141, M298, M300, R229, S902.
'Peredur'   A7,   B536,   B745,   B756,   C59,   C60,   D94,   D164,
F142, F231, G186, G188, G189, G190, G191, G193, G194, G195,
G222, G359, H150, J145, J254, L257, L626, L627, M18, M197,

<85>

M202, M663, M699, M700, M702, P343, P508, R206, R264, R397, R489, R492, S810, S845, W210, W211, W212, W426, W428, W429, Z30, Z33.
Pergamon F187.
Perilous Castle L508.
Perilous Chapel J145.
'Perlesvaus' A72, A194, B861, C49, C51, C55, C56, C202, D46, D177, E164, F248, F250, G15, G22, H185, H478, I18, K107, K108, K109, K351, K383, L393, L428, L564, L573, M203, M209, M723, N177, N186, N189, N190, N226, N230, N231, O21, O89, P151, P385, R313, R314, R365, R366, S184, S243, S508, S732, S840, S841, S951, T127, T283, V20, W134, W174, W203, W247, W265, W266, W270, W315, W425, W430, W433, W435, W442, W443, W515, W640, W640.
Persia P373.
Persian Epic Z28.
Persian Influence H393, L265, R117, R270, R467, S287, S444, S563, S903, W494, W498.
'Persibein'. See Ulrich Fueetrer.
Personal Names. See Names, Personal.
Personification K191, N156.
Peter von Staufenberg S283.
'Petit Artus de Bretagne'. See 'Arthur of Little Britain'.
Petitcru G172, K349.
Petrarch B355, C12.
 'Trionfi' B355, C11.
Petronius S7.
Petrus M470.
Peutinger, Table of S850.
Pfeiffer, Franz H542.
'Phantom's Frenzy (The)' O109.
Philip of Flanders A82, C59, D94, N199, N202, S760.
Philology H3, L361, S406.
'Philomena' A130, L299, L300.
Phoenician Origins W5.
Phoenix M18, W608.
Physiognomy P7.
'Physiologus' G364.
Picous T64.
Pierre de Blois   T100.
'Piers Plowman' F35, H91, S648.
Piety W610.
Pilgrimages H144, H307.
Pillow, Enchanted N135.
Pity W83.
Place Names. See Names, Place.
Plantagenets H188, S173.
Plato S494.
Platonism W278.
Pleier, Der R276, R277.
 'Garel von dem bluehenden Tal' B106, B562, H651, W90.
 'Meleranz' B106.

<86>

'Tandareis und Flordibel' B106, K154.
Poet (Function of) D183, F81.
Poetics A117, F476, R242, S726, U4, U5, U6, V68, V76, W278.
Poison C10.
Poitiers, The Court of G17.
Poland B647, S193.
Politics H5, M62, M478, P163, R110, T271.
Polydore Vergil H241, H242.
'Polyolbion' T192.
Pont de L'Epee M477.
Pont Evage W160.
'Ponthus et Sydoine' K154, S621.
'Porte' (Sublime) J46.
'Ponzela Gaia' A90, V16, V17, V18.
Pope Simplicius A226.
Popular Literature W507.
Portraits C283, S255.
Portugal M225, R245.
Portuguese D138, L78, M222, N88, R460.
Portuguese Arthurian Literature B507, E110, M85, M86, M600.
Portuguese Literature B242, B243, B484, B514, C41, D67,
E109, K224, L75, M175, M638, P185, R461, T97, T99.
 In England T98.
See also 'Demanda Do Santo Graal'.
Portuguese Lyric L163.
Portuguese Translation of Malory L129.
Potent Song C25.
Poverty and Riches B957.
Powys B94, E78.
Powys, John Cowper, 'A Glastonbury Romance' B764, G205.
Praemonstratensian Order M67.
Predestination B384, S319.
'Preideu Annwvyn' J102, R489.
Pre-Raphaelite Painters A211, I28.
'Presbys Ippotes' P368.
Prester John H326.
Pridwen H366.
Priest, Good S9.
'Primaleon' T98.
Princes of Wales J273.
'Princesse de Cleves' H394.
'Prison et Croisie'
'Privilegium Fori' A75.
Procession in Castle of Wonders M628.
Profanity O106, O108.
'Profecias de Sabio Merlin' T13.
See also Merlin.
Prologues J51, J52, K271, M498, M573, O55, P176, S717,
W247.
 Prologues of Chretien de Troyes F430, H637.
Prophecies B918, E160, E161, E162, F98, G157, G337, J259,

<87>

N25, W422, W510.
'Prophecy and the Eagle' L320.
Prophecy of the Dragons W413.
'Prophetia Merlini'. See 'Merlin, Prophetia' and Geoffrey
of Monmouth.
Prophetic Poems R209.
Prose   Romances   B33,   D228,   F320, F484, M330, N205, P257,
P340, S626, T151.
See also Grail and individual authors and titles.
Prose Romances (French). See French Prose Romances.
Prose Style H403.
Prosper of Aquitaine P63.
'Protheselaus' L145, S100.
Provencal C98, D124, E126, F299, G314, M607, N76, V12.
Provencal   Literature   B871, C31, C275, F185, J117, K287,
L223, L233, L366, N73, N74, N293, R149, R152, R394, S945.
See also 'Blandrin, Ensenhammer, 'Flamenca', 'Jaufre',
Troubadours.
Provencal Lyric A290, D127, J146, J149, M612.
Proverbs A130, B768, F354, H4, T208.
Prydain V25.
Pryderi J281.
Psalms S32, T42.
'Psautier Barberini, Le' S863.
Pseudo-Map C57, L614.
Pseudo-Robert de Boron   B471, P49, P276, S624, S628, V41,
W173, W304.
Pseudo-Wauchier B266, R325.
Psychoanalysis G260, M110.
Psychoanalytic Criticism H510.
Psychological Depth in Hartmann's 'Erec' H598.
Psychology B171, C348, J323, L121, P362, S366, S492.
'Pucelle As Manches Petites, La' F296.
Pucelle, La Mauvaise L160.
Pucci, Antonio S56.
Pulci, Luigi B258, F42, G116, G342, L250, R538, S36, S54,
W356, W357.
 'Morgante' A89, A91, B893, B952, B953, C71, C110, G136,
M131, M132, P298, P299, R36, S414, V10, W251.
'Pum Breuddwyd Gwenddydd' W63.
Punjab Legend B199.
Purcell, Henry H400.
'Purgatorio' L286.
Purgatory R274.
Purgatory of Saint Patrick M125, R274, S844.
'Purity' A18, L34, S691.
See also 'Cleanness'.
'Purse' S582.
Pwyll B56, C157, G187, L338, M16, N186, W10.
'Pwyll Pen Annwfn' L334, L335.

<88>

'Pwyll Pendeuic Dyuet'   'Pyramis and Thisbe'

Pwyll Pendeuic Dyuet (Prince of Dyfed)'   F460, I6, I7, M18,
S191, T133.
'Pyramis and Thisbe' B954, K237, R482, R558, S431.

<90>

Rabelais   C227, F345, F346.
Raimbaut d'Orange   D86.
Raimon de Miraval   T235..
Rain-making Spring   D195, L311, R387.
Raoul de Houdenc   F495, K22, K370, K454, K456, L713, M435,
T145, W265, Z27, Z68.
 'Meraugis de Portlesguez' A55, C26, F305, H616, K188, K370,
L459, O21, P156, S710.
 'Vengeance de Raguidel' A63, A65, C372, F495, G105, G106,
K389, M435, P3, P12, R392, R482, T142, T144, W265, W509.
Rape   H650.
Ravens   L668.
'Reali di Francia'   R540.
Realism   N158, R11, S482, S888.
Rebellion of the Kings   W524.
Recluses   M180.
'Reconoistre au Parler...'   M571.
'Recort de Victoire'   M75.
'Recreantise'   C169.
'Recueil des Hystoires Troyennes'   F432.
'Red Book of Hergest'   J238, J252, J289, L641, N285, R201,
R202, S364, T131, T133.
Red Knight   P8A.
Reinart   H254, H258, M731.
Redemption   G85, P152, W314.
'Reden und Schweigen'   R397.
Relics   D175.
Relics of the Passion   G150.
Religion   B228, B256, B947, B948, C170, F442, H389, H645,
K220, M40, M279, M330, P152, S4, S8, S71, S482, S745, S872,
V132, V133.
Religious Motifs   D282, H603, M176.
Renaissance Romance   B258, G136, J312.
Renart, Jean. See Jean Renart.
Renaud or Renaut de Beaujeau   F117, L243, L713.
 'Lai d'Ignaure'   L218, L243.
 'Libeaus Desconnus'   B429, B530, C333, D120, E174, F144,
H518, K23, M57. M386, M528, M533, M534, O113, S240, T259, W321,
W322, W373, W374.
See also Fair Unknown.
Renges de s'Espethe   L177.
'Renner, Der'   B671, B672, B673, G196, R526.
See also Hugo von Trimberg.
'Rennewart'   E48.
See also Ulrich von Tuerheim.
Repentance   B256, G22, P149, P152, P155, T85.
Rex Inutilis   K129, P213.
'Rey Mabun'   B896.
Reymes, William   K46.
Reynard the Fox   R112, T245.
Rhan Gyntfa, 'Y Seint Greal'   J203.

<91>

Rheged   M681.
Rheims, Council of   D130.
'Rhetorica ad Herennium'   L717.
Rhetoric   C193, H635, H636, L315, M527, O108, S194.
Rhiannon   G398.
'Rhonabwy, Dream of'.   See 'Dream of Rhonabwy'.
Rhuthin   J285.
'Rhwng Chwedl A Chredo'   D36.
Rhymes   D99.
'Ricardian Poetry'   B936.
'Richard Coeur de Lion'   S881.
Richard I of England   B771, D2, D176, S591.
Richard II of England   R254.
Richard de Fournival   T100.
Richard Fitz Gilbert   L336.
Richard of Cirencester   R46, T238, W333.
Richard of Ireland   B857, B859, O28, P121.
  'Prophecies de Merlin'   B858, B858A, M108, O28, P121.
'Richars Li Biaus'   P401.
Richeut   K5, K7.
Richter, Werner   S653.
'Riddere Metter Mouwen'   H5, J309, K426, P401.
'Ridder Metter Swane'   F173.
Rigaut de Barbezieux   L231, L237, L238, R512, V20.
'Rigomer, Les Merveilles de'. See 'Merveilles de Rigomer'.
Rimbaud, Arthur   C223.
'Ring of the Dove'.   See Ibn Hazm.
Rions, King   R524.
'Riot' in the Alliterative 'Morte Arthure'   G373.
Rishanger, William   K51, K52.
Ritson, Joseph   D120, H551, R304.
Ritual   H546, W275.
Ritualistic Tasks   T53.
'Ritual To Romance'   B399, W275.
River Dee   H364.
River Names   B417.
See also Names, Place; and Onomastics.
Riwalin   C219.
Robert, Brother   E141.
See also Tristan (Scandinavian).
Robert de Blois   F318.
Robert de Boron   A75, A76, B30, B529, B867, C50, G20, H439, H441, H617, I18, K82, K282, L168, L612, M183, M185, M450, M452, N180, N181, N195, N197, N211, N227, P276, R513, S626, S627.
  'Merlin'   G135, M446, M455, M478, M486, O30, P49, P151, W312.
  'Estoire dou Graal'   G135, K120, M470, N227, S42.
  Prose 'Joseph d'Arimathie'   A75, A76, C106, H607, M448, M486, O27, O31, O33, O34, P152, R319, W192.
See also Pseudo-Robert de Boron.
Robert de Torigny   H532.

<92>

'Robert Le Diable' R74, W557.
Robert of Gloucester B795.
Roberts, Dorothy James, 'The Enchanted Cup' W327.
Robin Hood P105.
Robinson, Edward Arlington A49, A67, A210, A234, B215, B216, C111, C217, C428, C429, D25, D44, F515, F533, H491, H611, L387, L650, M659, N69, P201, P202, P204, R121.
  'Tristram' C430, F323, N69, P201.
'Rodlieb' W484.
Rohal H566.
Roi Mehaigne. See Maimed Kings.
Roi-Pecheur A134, D93, F442, K7, V32.
See also Castles and Fisher King.
Roland G278.
'Roland' L303.
See also 'Chanson de Roland'
'Roland Furious' M294, P409.
See also Ariosto and 'Orlando Furioso'.
Roman Britain A206, B723, C158, C289, G338, H624, J13, M760, M762, P69, R537, S350, S943, W23, W538, Z3.
'Roman de la Rose' G439, H253, K313, M63, P163.
'Roman de la Violette'. See Gerard de Nevers.
'Roman de Silence'. See Heldris de Cornualle.
'Roman de Thebes' D99, G358, H456.
'Roman de Troie' C366.
'Roman du Graal', (Post-Vulgate). See Grail and Pseudo-Robert de Boron
Romance B218, E136, G360, H38, H438, H564, M474, V72, V78.
See also Arthurian Romances and individual countries.
Romance Languages and Literatures, Bibliography F159.
Romance Lyric E125.
Romance Philology H567, H569.
Romanesque B153, P340.
Romano-Celtic Frontier R537.
Rome L289, M139.
Ron (Arthur's Lance) H366, L414, W137, W137.
Ronsard F341.
'Ronwen ou Rhonwen' W420.
Roques, Mario F401, L235, N277.
Ross, Alan S. C. J272.
Rossetti, Dante Gabriel T287.
'Rota Veneris' F224.
Rotte (Musical Instrument) S786.
'Rou' (Roman de). See Wace.
'Roue Arzur (Ar)' L62.
Rougemont, Denis de W281.
Round Table A188, A193, B60, B379, B382, B615, B616, B622, B685, B686, B779, C137, D23, D102, D104, D130, D182, D237, D274, D285, E1, E142, F71, F114, F236, F414, F435, G160, G261, G359, G383, G429, H165, H457, H584, H626, J168, J216, K106, L147, L472, L473, L476, L502, L540, L581, M225, M381,

<93>

M450, M452, M674, N124, P38, P50, P71, P350, R172, R220, R308, R396, S147, S332, S413, S432, S704, T90, T205, W193, W254, W273, W285, W345, W361, Z87.
Rousecouane T150.
Royalty C308, J29.
'Rudolf von Ems' B634, K11.
 'Willehalm' H227, H228.
Ruiz, Juan M81, R517.
Rumanian Literature C83.
Rummaret de Wenelande W595.
Runkelstein Frescoes T182, W90.
Ruse J331.
Russian Literature P109, S179.
Rustichello da Pisa B483, G420, L91, L92, L438, M493, P259.
 'Roman du Roi Artus' B492.
See also Guiron le Courtois and 'Palamede'.
'Ryence's Challenge, King' F490.

<94>

Sachs, Hans G166, S158, S599, S600.
Sacred Stones T73.
Sadism in Layamon B410.
'Saga og Sprak' W209.
Saga B71, D14, H352, K21, K415, L668, T220.
Sagremor G18, K294, S928.
Sahagun R245.
Saint-Duzec D277.
'Saint Erkenwald' K333.
Saint Michael's Mount. See Mont Saint-Michel.
Saints in 'Sir Gawain and the Green Knight' T4.
Saints' Legends C361, L547.
Saints' Lives   A146, A246, B265, B763, B925, C124, C398,
D18, D195, D196, D198, D199, E122, F29, H121, H161, H165, H363,
L259, L328, L329, L339, L464, M670, P22, R105, R206, S181,
S810, S812, S950, T22, T26, T28, T63, T75, W12, W13, W21, W119,
W140.
See also Breton, Celtic, Cornish, Welsh, and individual names.
Sala, Pierre M713, S923.
 'Tristan' M509, M712, M714, M722.
'Salade, La' K182.
'Salesbieres, La Bataille de' F422.
Salisbury, John of C367.
Sampson, Saint D177.
'Samson The Fair' L125.
'San', Meaning of M359.
'Sank Ryal' F528, M486.
See also Grail.
Sarrasin, Jehan, 'Roman de Hem' H329.
Satire M478, S258, S471.
See also Humour.
Savage H618.
Saxo Grammaticus L664, S552, T214.
Saxon Conquest B723, C289, H408, M760, R103, S344.
Saxons C132, J286, L663, W658, Z3.
Scandinavian Arthurian Literature T214, T218.
Scandinavian Ballads S121.
Scandinavian Folktales C194, S121.
Scandinavian Influence J225, P243, R147, T221, Z72.
Scandinavian Literature F349, H385, H648, L125, L697, M563,
S121.
Scandinavian Myth R410, T53, V132.
Scandinavian Religion M23.
Scandinavian Versions T220.
Schaeffer, Albrecht, 'Parzival' I1.
Schanpfanzun M261.
Schastel G198.
Schinderhannes G166.
Schionatulander W624, W630.
Schirmer, W. P292.
School of Chartres W278.

<95>

Schools A130.
Schroeder, Franz Rolf R68.
Schroeder, W. J. R528.
Schuecking, Levin L. H12.
Schulz, Albert, 'San Marte' G327, P234.
'Schwanritter'. See Konrad von Wuerzburg, Lohengrin, and
Wagner.
Schwietering, Julius B360.
Scilly H317.
Scotland B408, B746, C118, C132, D185, D186, G121, G122,
G179, L182, L185, L554, R303, S703.
Scott, Sir Walter E21, M44, P267.
Scottish Ballads G276, W537.
Scottish Chronicles G179.
Scottish Gaelic S412.
Scottish History E187.
Scottish Literature C380, S574.
Scottish Tradition D227, S700.
Scribal Editing K135, S899.
Scribes C168.
Scriptural Pattern K104.
Secchi, Nicolo K46.
'Seege of Troye' (Middle English Romance) B350,   H490.
See also Troy, Troyes.
Segontium L528.
Segramor M286.
'Sen' H646, K300.
Seneca M269.
Seneschals H606, W581.
'Sente Mey(e)' C368, L362.
Sentimentality A137, B36, B890.
'Sergas de Esplandian' G146.
Serglige con Culainn D162.
Serpent P42.
Setmunt L289.
'Seven Sages of Rome' K365.
Sexual Intemperance G383.
Sexuality L121, P339.
'Seyn Graal' F528, M486.
'Sgel Isgaide Leithe' D241.
Shadow King. See Rex Inutilis.
Shakespeare B342, C161, K46, L87, L111, L113, L114, M316,
N62, N224, P381.
Shape-shifting L456.
Shaw, James E. G242.
'Siabhradh Mhic na Miochomhairle' (The Enchantment of the
Son of Bad Counsel) C67, C69.
Sibyl Tradition K181, K182.
Sicily H349, H350, S173.
Sidney, Philip, 'Arcadia' G209.

<96>

'Sieffre o Fynwy' J99.
Siege Perilous N223.
'Siesa-Sessoyne' M241.
Sigifrid L161.
Sigune G364, L5, M408, W624, W630.
'Sigune auf der Linde' G364.
Sigurd A239, G278, S410.
Silence R192, R397, T143.
'Silence, Le Roman de'. See Heldris de Cornualle.
Silimac W246.
Silvester   J173.
Simcox, George Augustus M155.
Sin B444.
'Sin Hochvart-Swindens Tac' L436.
Sinadon L528.
'Sir Galahad'. See Galahad, and Tennyson.
'Sir Gawain and the Green Knight'. See 'Gawain and the Green
Knight'.
'Sir Launfal'. See Chestre, Thomas.
Sire F249.
Siren L268.
'Six Old English Chronicles' G285.
Sleeping King Myth B813.
Snjofrid G267.
'Snjofridar Drapa' H55.
Snorri T53.
Snowdon L530.
Social Life J299, L361.
Social Problems   B957, F54, G184, G197, G407, H184, H477,
K53, M519, R67, R526, S349, S388.
Sociology   B649, C170, C299, F298, H5, K292, K293, L358,
M364, M369, P214, V32, W152.
'Sohrab and Rustem' P380.
Solomon D32, L120, W243.
See also Uevre Salemun.
'Solomon and Asmodeus' T152.
Solomon's Ship Q6.
'Somnium Scipionis' L685.
'Sone de Nausay' C183, G211, K301, L496, L548, M203, N297,
P156.
'Song of Songs' B468, L251.
'Songe de l'Arbre' B643.
'Songe de Paradis' M435.
Sorcerer S562, W45, Z89.
Source Studies L589, L590, L591, L593, L596, L623, P342.
Sources D14, E65, K75, L468, L523, M106, P30, P31, S187,
T208, W170, W171.
South Cadbury A113, A114, G350.
South Cadbury Castle. See Castles.
Southern Influences L221.

<97>

Sovereignty A54, A56, H650.
'Spagna' C92, V100.
Spain B517, L275, R245, S34.
Spanish Cancioneros G308.
Spanish Indies L252.
Spanish Influence R243.
Spanish Lyric L163.
Spanish Literature B89, B300, B513, B514, B515, B621, B629,
C390, E106, E107, E108, E109, E110, K123, K224, L252, M84, M85,
M247, N269, P115, P284, P285, P286, R180, R245, R282, R407,
R518, S461, T97, T99.
 Medieval A127, B485, B518, B519, B520, B554, H189, M86,
R284.
See also 'Demanda del Sancto Grial'; Grail Legend
(Spanish version); Tristan (Spanish).
Spanish Material in English Literature K372.
Spanish Novella R283.
Sparrow-Hawk Episode W244.
Spenser, Edmund   A121, A273, B257, B258, B641, B887, D43,
D313, E80, E131, E143B, F313, F461, G312, H47, H623, K115,
L247, M287, M310, M709, N62, P279, R71, R121, R173, S816, S820,
S932, T137, T282, W89, W145, W223, W674, Y2.
 'Faerie Queene' A194, A241, A256, A273, B259, B281, B385,
B641, B887, C148, D310, D313, E158, E159, F43, F307, G33, G136,
G318, G319, G444, H90, H91, H92, H93, H263, H322, H549, H623,
J239, J240, K115, L111, M520, M523, M524, N62, N70, O113, O118,
P55, P56, P381, P391, R173, R237, R378, S368, S369, S433, S441,
S583, S708, S734, T173, T236, W89, W553, W647, Y2.
'Spicilegium Vaticanum' F172.
'Spoils of Annawn' L566.
Springs, Sacred M156.
'Spruch von den Tafelrundern' M381.
'Squyer Meldrum' R260.
St. Albans L283.
St. David's B763.
'St. Trudperter Hohenlied' R395.
Stag of Love R72, T86.
Stag, White. See White Stag.
Stake, Vacant T45.
'Stanzas of the Graves' W379.
Steinbeck, John G36.
Stereotype Formulae in Old French H609.
Sterility R192.
Stewart, John of Baldynneis M294, P409.
Stockholm L52.
Stone and Ring of Eluned T95.
Stone of Destiny N223.
Stonehenge H154, H156, L477, L478, S889.
Storm-making Springs H94.
See also Barenton, Fountain of; and Chretien de Troyes,
'Yvain'.

<98>

Strategy D24, R94.
Strathclyde C221.
Strathclyder H655.
'Strengleikar' H52, K159, S540.
Stricker, Der B26, B562, S171.
Strongbow L178, L336.
Structure B154, B282, F208, G27, H412, K202, L279, M134, M477, S475, S722.
Structure of Romances H223, W507.
Structural Comparison A59.
Structural Studies A117, C76, C288, D308, K63, M575, P247, S532, W224, W341.
Studies in Honour of. See Festschriften.
Style B158, B256, B390, G263, K249.
Stylistic Problems B659.
Stylistics B153, B458, C106, C283, C348, C411, D317, F411, F413, F442, F481, G106, G181, H66, H219, H312, J161, M128, M330, R85, R192, S480, S947, W125, Z94.
Substantival Adjective C214.
Suende H305.
Suffering, Theme of C179.
Suhtscheck, Friedrich von S933, S934, U10, U11.
Suibhne Geilt C64, J10, J104.
'Suite du Merlin'. See Merlin.
Sul-Minerva C410.
'Summer Sunday' G62, T276.
Sunken Cities N263.
Supernatural C39, C40, C96, F118, G250, J305, S29.
Suso, Heinrich B381.
Sverrir D14.
Swan B285.
Swan Knight B91, B443, C382, F480, G228, H472, K425, P341, S374.
See also Konrad von Wuerzburg, Lohengrin, and Wagner.
Swedish Legendary C416.
Swedish Literature B411, N257, N258.
Swinburne, Algernon C. C217, J246, M703, R121, W620.
  'Tale of Balen' D220.
  'Tristram of Lyonesse' M703.
Swiss Literature E119, G328, N3, S522.
Sword G356, S319, W51.
Sword Bridge S29.
Sword of Mercy D176, D177.
Sword Test M436.
Symbolic Boar T84.
Symbolism B403, C143, C253, D317, F35, F415, F425, G28, G165, G454, H221, H248, H636, L13, L90, L287, L460, L613, L617, L691, L692, M558, M614, R59, R72, R116, R323, R535, S306, S489, S544, S757, T37, T38, T241, W56, W57, W287, W389.
Symbols B438, B669, E67, F73, F440, K325, L331, R192, S66,

<99>

<100>

<101>

<102>

<103>

K123, K146, K276, K303, K321, K355, K380, K405, K433, K434, K435, K450, K455, L39, L40, L41, L94, L144, L165, L181, L227, L236, L239, L261, L265, L273, L364, L435, L462, L465, L466, L535, L566, L647, L654, L679, M39, M99, M100, M162, M189, M207, M267, M292, M320, M349, M351, M391, M444, M485, M509, M545, M588, M606, M618, M659, M661, N66, N91, N145, N148, N153, N156, N157, N167, N254, O91, O111, P27, P45, P109, P165, P182, P243, P274, P349, P350, R29, R55, R59, R72, R112, R390, R418, R460, R523, R540, S69, S74, S76, S121, S127, S165, S170, S294, S332, S343, S384, S398, S446, S452, S521, S566, S581, S599, S600, S633, S654, S697, S728, S883, S935, T8, T253, T261, V21, V22, V24, V47, W91, W116, W125, W151, W179, W296, W306, W327, W372, W402, W403, W529, W620, W625, Z91.

See also Arnold, Matthew; Bedier; Beroul; Eilhart von Oberg; 'Folie Tristan'; Gottfried von Strassburg; Immermann; Marie de France,'Chevrefeuille'; Robinson, E. A.; Sala; Thomas of Britain; Ulrich von Tuerheim; and Wagner.

Tristan Legend B50, B89, B308, B309, B653, B666, B739, B839, B845, B850, C10, C66, C101, C144, C181, C199, C335, C445, D12, D70, D84, D85, D111A, D177, D284, E65, E144, F242, F278, F338, G172, G217, G218, G220, G221, G227, G231, H71, H224, H319, H320, H540, J67, J127, K68, K69, K278, K349, K351, K409, K451, L122, L356, L468, L486, L487, L488, L491, L495, L610, L628, L629, M387, M595, M660, M687, M744, N141, N143, N149, N269, P210, R50, R61, R133, R244, R256, R308, R452, R480, R481, R484, S143, S159, S179, S220, S287, S375, S377, S539A, S544, S722, S929, T175, T245, T260, W309, W386, Y11, Z28, Z65.

Early Tristan Poems W311.

Episodic Tristan Poems T66.

'Tristan' (Breton) L63.

(Czech) B955, J59, K242, K243, K244.

(Danish) S176.

(English, Middle) D171.

(French Poems) B732, G229.

(French Prose) A66, A164, B149, B150, B151, B153, B200, B261, B262, B405, B473, B476, B477, B480, B486, B499, B549, B552, B824, C146, C353, C441, C442, C443, C444, C446, D102, F58, F59, F235, G229, G249, G358, H378, H645, J163, J164, J298, K128, K135, L91, L148, L234, L422, L423, L437, L438, L439, L440, M73, M75, M188, M715, M717, M749, O29, P44, P144, P147, P158, P197, P271, R131, S30, S151, S417, S434, S471, S541, S621, S625, S842, T213, V21, V51, V52, V53, V69, V73, V74, V76, V78, W115, W542.

(German Prose) B660, C204, F516, K279, K422, S930.

See also individual authors.

(Italian) D102, D103, D104, L159, S432.

See also 'Cantari di Tristano' and 'Tristano Riccardiano'.

(Low Frankish) S564.

(Modern Cornish Version) S570.

(Modern English Version) B209, H215.

<104>

(Modern French Version) A207, B346, B598, C145, C146, G73,
G451, M111, M214, M215, M217, P244, R131, S570.
See also Bedier.
(Modern German Version) B210, W335.
(Modern Irish Version) P244.
(Modern Italian Version) B52, V39.
(Old Serbian) R10.
(Portuguese) P191.
(Primitive Version) C244, D83, V21.
(Slavic) B49.
(Spanish) A232, B153, B554, K123, L399, N267, N268, N269,
N629, P182, R284, S417, T270, W62.
(Welsh) C418, J213, L577, W399.
'Tristan de Nanteuil' B862, K376, S512.
'Tristan Le Bret' (La Grande Histoire de) A10, J164.
'Tristan Menestrel' B214.
'Tristan Moine' B951.
'Tristano Corsiniano' A135, A136, G8.
'Tristano Riccardiano'   D102, D104, H165, P58, R540, S432,
W358.
'Ystoria Trystan' L624, L625, L627.
'Tristan's Madness, Tale of' F60.
'Tristany, El' A235.
Tristfardd J263.
Tristram's Sword D176, D177.
'Tristrams Saga'. See Brother Robert.
'Tristrant' E24, E25.
'Tristrem, Sir' (Middle English)   H540, K110, K298, K395,
L455, M306, M318, P267, R29, R520, S127, S917, V115, V116, Y8,
Y9, Y11.
Triuwe, The Meaning of B398.
'Troilus' B936, F310, M219, T248.
Trojan Legend   A227, F26, F103, F432, G240, H252, H254,
L432, M234, P102, P297, W579.
See also Troy, Troyes.
'Tromdamh Guaire' J321.
Troncq B167.
Troubadour Love P307, V13.
Troubadour Lyric K287, V110.
Troubadour Poetry C241, C242, L231.
Troubadours   A163, A290, B110, B143, B291, B334, B620,
B714, C98, D91, D124, D128, D129, D131, D139, D319, E8, F76,
F357, F502, G308, H362, I3, J118, J119, K185, K292, K321, L20,
L161, L218, L227, L232, L238, L308, L366, L458, M60, M163,
M374, N74, N88, N290, N291, N292, P186, P187, P245, P293, P365,
R279, R381, R502, S144, S145, S657, S896, S944, V20, V127,
V128, W218, W279.
Trouveres. See Troubadours.
Troy, Troyes C261, F507, H535.
See also Trojan Legend.

<105>

<106>

<107>

<108>

G63, H134, J192, K114, K184, K345, K348, K350, K351, P124, P384, R103, S943, W8, W30, W34, W413.
Vortigern's Tower B225.
Vortimer A239.
Vostaert, Penninc en Pieter, 'Walewein en het Schaakboord' E137.
Voyage G260, J305, M363, S28, S722.
'Voyage of Saint Brendan'. See Brendan, Saint.
'Voyage d'Outremer' J46.
Voyage, Theme of the Marvellous F254, H220.
'Vray Gargantua' F347, K182.
Vremede Hirz G386.
'Vreude' in Hartmann von Aue E124.
'Vrou Minne' G86.
Vulgate Cycle B384, B477, C57, F398, H185, H260, J2, K245, L280, L595, M366, P3, P50, P255, S164, S626, S630, S864, T104, T213, T283, Z92.
See also 'Lancelot' (French Prose).
'Vulgate Merlin'. See Merlin.
Vulgate Romances A76, B221, B611, F223, F373, M442, N198, R150, R396, S630, T194, W325.

<109>

<110>

Wauchier B861.
See also Pseudo-Wauchier.
Wauchier de Denain B851, M426, M462, P175, W258.
'Perceval' L86.
Weapons A12, A121, C50, D9, D226, H366, L108, W232.
See also Excalibur.
Weapons, Magic E149.
Weber, Gottfried B360, R528.
'Weddynge of Syr Gawain and Dame Ragnell'. See 'Gawain,
Marriage of'.
Wells, Holy J224, M156.
Welsh B173, E160, E161, E162, F229, G337, H83, H108, H524,
J16, J80, J81, J212, J221, J260, L314, L319, L320, L321, L345,
L407, L410, L411, L520, L524, M32, N131, N199, P1, R200, R330,
R353, S896, V109, W411, W434.
Welsh Arthur J199.
Welsh Arthurian Romances J253.
Welsh Bards B755, M137, M662.
Welsh Biography D152.
Welsh 'Bruts'. See 'Brut'.
Welsh Folklore R186.
Welsh Genealogies B98, B101, B103, C125, J222.
Welsh History B95, C100, C125, L402A, R380, W363.
Welsh Influence in Renaissance England M523, M524.
Welsh Influence on Chretien G193.
Welsh Law E84, F216, R204, R205, W445.
Welsh Legends J105, J106, J242, J250, J258, S832, S833,
S834, S835, S836, T101, W415.
Welsh Literature A224, B735, B742, C137, C187, C188, C418,
D36, D243, E75, E84, E156, E163, F27, F219, G2, G222, G273,
G274, G353, G355, G394, G397, H72, H79, H159, H495, H667, J22,
J88, J93, J105, J107, J195, J209, J210, J213, J217, J233, J234,
J235, J238, J254, J257, J262, J263, J264, J279, J281, J288,
L318, L322, L333, L340, L346, L355, L403, L498, L530, L531,
M136, M662, M669, O75, P59, P60, P61, P64, P69, P73, P99, P100,
P292, P346, R182, R201, R209, R340, R343, R348, R352, R380,
S546, S553, S646, S845, S846, W21, W22, W70, W376, W378, W379,
W394, W395, W397, W399, W402, W403, W404, W412, W418, W422.
Welsh Literature, History of P98.
Welsh Minstrels B899.
Welsh Nationalism W37.
Welsh Origin of the Arthurian Legend M617.
Welsh Place Names P240.
Welsh Princes P70.
Welsh Saints B763, C124, D198, R206, S950.
Welsh Songs L341.
Welsh Tradition B738, B751, B755, B780, G194, J24, J25,
O110, R107, S590.
Welsh Versions R335, T248.
Werewolf B118, D300.
Wernher der Gartenaere, 'Meier Helmbrecht' T263.

<111>

<112>

Wolff, Ludwig S326.
Wolfram von Eschenbach A9, A69, A76, A77, A142, A146,
A202, A249, B19, B23, B24, B25, B26, B46, B108, B145, B159,
B189, B219, B296, B362, B364, B465, B467, B467A, B467A, B470,
B599, B600, B609, B720, B724, B889, D75, D140, D166, E26, E27,
E39, E40, E41, E91, E92, E103, E185, E186, F14, F61, F125,
F146, F211, F294, F358, F485, F504, G40, G82, G83, G92, G126,
G170, G197, G199, G200, G202, G224, G225, G226, G265, G325,
G348, G401, G413, H25, H45, H46, H108, H167, H170, H175, H198,
H199, H201, H202, H204, H206, H213, H214, H232, H251, H265,
H271, H278, H297, H298, H313, H339, H473, H486, H487, H552,
H553, H562, H573, H597, I35, J36, J68, J76, J132, J196, J228,
J310, K12, K58, K77, K78, K79, K80, K112, K113, K167, K200,
K203, K226, K236, K262, K263, K264, K308, K328, K332, K340,
K354, K403, K421, K428, K457, K462, L5, L85, L88, L202, L204,
L209, L212, L441, L453, L587, L702, L704, M53, M126, M127,
M167, M255, M257, M263, M323, M327, M350, M390, M392, M393,
M396, M420, M546, M553, M569, M578, M648, M649, M652, M658,
M686, M687, M705, M706, M754, N41, N43, N45, N55, N72, N84,
N102, N109, N114, N115, N119, N165, N261, O87, P21, P29, P133,
P252, P318, P322, P323, P324, P325, P327, P330, R19, R42, R51,
R56, R59, R121, R213, R214, R215, R216, R217, R218, R221, R226,
R240, R377, R388, R393, R404, R405, R441, R450, R451, R456,
R528, R535, S71, S73, S130, S206, S252, S253, S254, S260, S264,
S275, S295, S298, S299, S303, S310, S312, S314, S317, S323,
S328, S329, S330, S334, S346, S349, S359, S371, S395, S396,
S399, S401, S403, S435, S447, S488, S511, S518, S591, S675,
S716, S735, S737, S739, S752, S753, S754, S764, S765, S895,
T62, T76, T80, T230, T243, T262, W38, W52, W65, W82, W83, W92,
W147, W158, W180, W182, W183, W191, W197, W235, W236, W240,
W338, W354, W501, W566, W567, W609, W613, W622, W624, W630,
W641, W642, Z25, Z40, Z43, Z44, Z45, Z79.
  Bibliography B906, P399.
  Imagery in T11, T12.
  'Parzival' A11, A68, A70, A77, A132, A166, A276, B25, B104,
B105, B145, B159, B168, B174, B180, B195, B219, B255, B296,
B326, B352, B375, B398, B414, B450, B451, B466, B468, B469,
B541, B542, B601, B602, B603, B604, B607, B632, B633, B835,
B866, B902, B906, C7, C36, C63, C296, C435, C436, C440, D5,
D18, D69, D93, D142, D167, D168, D205, D267, D282, E20, E22,
E26, E29, E31, E34, E46, E49, E50, E56, E58, E67, E132, E134,
F3, F55, F81, F83, F86, F102, F282, F284, F290, F293, F295,
F296, F297, F335, F336, F480, F485, F486, F501, G5, G29, G85,
G96, G125, G163, G166, G173, G188, G198, G304, G306, G341,
G364, G365, G366, G367, G368, G376, G378, G388, G391, G442, H7,
H8, H9, H29, H120, H143, H171, H172, H174, H176, H187, H200,
H205, H211, H221, H227, H251, H264, H267, H281, H287, H290,
H293, H305, H313, H314, H315, H327, H328, H336, H337, H339,
H347, H359, H393, H395, H476, H480, H481, H482, H483, H484,
H485, H487, H488, H554, H556, H557, H558, H561, H562, H563,
H589, H597, H604, H618, H661, H669, I31, I35, J28A, J34, J55,

<113>

J56, J64, J77, J140, J168, J169, J170, J171, J172, J176, J177,
J178, J196, J226, J248, J316, K2, K4, K5, K6, K7, K8, K9, K16,
K38, K54, K55, K56, K57, K152, K161, K167, K199, K204, K205,
K206, K207, K228, K230, K251, K252, K253, K256, K260, K263,
K275, K283, K295, K309, K312, K315, K316, K317, K319, K322,
K330, K341, K400, K401, K402, K404, K410, K418, K425, K429,
K430, K432, K444, K446, K452, K459, K460, K467, K471, L7, L8,
L10, L51, L85, L119, L153, L170, L194, L198, L203, L205, L208,
L211, L213, L214, L316, L351, L354, L386, L388, L436, L441,
L442, L444, L446, L447, L450, L645, L651, L660, L661, L662,
L704, M53, M65, M66, M167, M252, M261, M264, M276, M286, M297,
M378, M380, M390, M392, M393, M397, M406, M421, M489, M544,
M569, M579, M580, M581, M582, M583, M584, M586, M589, M590,
M591, M592, M597, M652, M689, M690, M705, M738, M757, N7, N44,
N72, N79, N80, N81, N82, N83, N115, N238, N239, N276, O38, O39,
O46, O72, O84, O85, O98, P4, P13, P26, P30, P32, P34, P148,
P177, P318, P324, P326, P328, P329, P331, P366, P397, P398, Q1,
Q8, R4, R59, R93, R142, R169, R222, R224, R228, R232, R233,
R234, R235, R236, R245, R264, R291, R397, R444, R454, R455,
R463, R516, R530, R532, R535, S4, S17, S128, S129, S140, S155,
S156, S168, S169, S201, S204, S206, S208, S210, S213, S216,
S228, S229, S231, S249, S256, S262, S269, S270, S274, S286,
S288, S295, S296, S297, S300, S301, S302, S305, S306, S308,
S309, S313, S315, S316, S319, S320, S321, S324, S325, S333,
S334, S358, S371, S392, S399, S404, S437, S444, S447, S487,
S489, S490, S510, S516, S517, S526, S527, S591, S653, S696,
S712, S715, S724, S732, S741, S743, S744, S745, S766, S767,
S768, S769, S771, S772, S773, S778, S779, S780, S799, S870,
S902, S918, S933, S934, S953, S954, T39, T41, T43, T44, T61,
T102, T196, T204, T207, T231, T233, U9, U10, U11, V126, W50,
W52, W80, W81, W82, W83, W85, W86, W87, W93, W96, W100, W148,
W149, W153, W157, W170, W171, W181, W186, W190, W194, W195,
W196, W197, W198, W202, W214, W219, W220, W224, W225, W227,
W236, W239, W342, W346, W349, W355, W453, W454, W456, W458,
W462, W464, W465, W466, W467, W472, W476, W477, W479, W481,
W494, W495, W496, W497, W498, W499, W506, W558, W559, W560,
W565, W574, W598, W605, W623, W626, W630, W649, W666, W677,
W678, W679, Z2, Z26, Z41, Z42, Z45, Z61, Z62, Z63, Z75, Z76.
See also Parzival, Perceval.
  'Titurel' B104, B105, B905, B906, B907, F36, F297, G38, H288,
H290, H291, H292, L8, L200, L215, M167, M170, M596, M689,
O37, O38, P335, R23, R225, R226, R503, S272, S309, S505, S510,
S742, S744, U12, W50, W189, W682.
  'Willehalm' B180, B902, C315, F335, F337, G401, H227, K265,
L215, L391, L392, L442, M53, M406, M706, M738, O36, P108, P334,
R236, S132, S309, S318, S331, S371, W152, W214, W623, W682.
  Works L9, M245.
Women in Romances B152, B605, B669, C63, F73, F524, G93,
G190, G352, G400, G436, H234, H605, J298, K44, K452, L160,
L234, L242, M143, M654, M674, M675, P156, R130, R349, S349,
S473, S782, W167, W542, W650.
Women's Costume C433, G176.

<114>

<115>

<116>

<117>